PRIMARY DIRECTIONS

ASTROLOGY'S OLD MASTER TECHNIQUE

Martin Gansten

The Wessex Astrologer

Published in 2009 by
The Wessex Astrologer Ltd
4A Woodside Road
Bournemouth
BH5 2AZ
England

www.wessexastrologer.com

ISBN 9781902405391

A catalogue record of this book is available at The British Library

Cover design by Dave at Creative Byte, Poole, Dorset

Unless otherwise stated in the text, astrological charts produced from
Solar Fire Deluxe v.6.0 by Esoteric Technologies Pty Ltd.

Cover credit: Portrait of Ptolemy, c.1475 (panel) by Joos van Gent
(Joos van Wassenhove) (fl.1460-75)
Louvre, Paris, France/Giraudon/The Bridgeman Art Library

For Anna

Preface

The painting on the cover of this book depicts Ptolemy, classical authority on primary directions, holding a model of the celestial sphere. We see him through the eyes of the Dutch artist Justus van Gent (c. 1410 – c. 1480), known today as an Old Master – a broad term used to designate painters of great technical skill, belonging to the European tradition, from the late Middle Ages up to the 18th century. Old Masters were accomplished craftsmen who discovered important principles of light, perspective, and composition. They belonged to an era in which art had not yet become wholly subjective, but was meant to represent an objective reality, whether physical or spiritual.

The ancient art of astrology, too, flourished in Europe from late medieval times throughout the Renaissance – surviving into the 18th century at least in Britain – and its foremost practitioners are well deserving of the epithet Old Masters. Among the techniques which they developed and refined in order to predict objectively real events, that of primary directions is perhaps most worthy of admiration – in the words of Jean-Baptiste Morin, *totius astrologiæ præcipuus ac divinissimus*, 'principal and most divine of all astrology'. This craft of the Old Masters can still be learnt – is, in fact, more easily acquired with the modern aids of calculators and computers, although it must be remembered that these are only tools for calculation and not substitutes for understanding. The subject is demanding, but not as forbidding or inaccessible as is often believed.

The few works on primary directions which have appeared in the last century, and of which even fewer are generally available today, have sometimes deterred readers by seeming to have been designed by mathematicians for mathematicians. In this book I have endeavoured to explain the principles of direction without recourse to trigonometrical formulae. The only knowledge presupposed in the reader is a basic acquaintance with the elements of astrology: the seven traditional planets, twelve signs and twelve houses.

For readers who want to try their hand at trigonometry, however, the necessary formulae are given in an appendix. Here, too, I have tried to clarify *what* is being done before explaining *how* to do it. Nevertheless, some experience in using a scientific calculator is helpful in order to follow the instructions; and I recommend going through the book itself before setting to work on the mathematical procedures in the appendix.

I have also attempted to shed light on the subject of directions by outlining their historical origins and development, both in the chapter specifically devoted to history and wherever relevant throughout the book. To this end, apart from English-language texts, I have made use of sources in Greek, Latin and German. Translations, unless otherwise stated, are mine.

A note on zodiacs: the Alexandrian originators of horoscopic astrology, and of the technique that developed into primary directions, used a fixed or sidereal zodiac. In the western branch of the astrological tradition this zodiac was gradually replaced, during late antiquity and the early Middle Ages, by the moving or tropical zodiac (while the Indian branch of the tradition remained sidereal). Directions as such are not dependent on either zodiac, but have been used with both. Readers may continue using whichever zodiac they are most familiar with; or they may wish to experiment, as house rulerships and dignities will change with the zodiac used. Personally, I have found the sidereal zodiac to give more reliable results than the tropical. The charts discussed in this book, except where taken from the works of older authors, have been calculated using a sidereal zodiac (with the precessional value, or *ayanāṃśa*, of K. S. Krishnamurti) and Alcabitius houses – for many centuries the most widespread quadrant house system, and the one favoured by my experience.

Finally, it is my pleasant duty to thank all those who have helped in bringing this book about, by giving valuable suggestions, patiently answering questions and discussing various technical points, or assisting in hunting down and deciphering obscure texts and references. Thanks are due to Erna Ahlfors, Philip Graves, Anton Grigoryev, Jan Hogendijk, James Holden, Deborah Houlding, Rumen Kolev, Ken Lee, Robert Nagy, Petr Radek and Ola Wikander, and especially to Thomas Decker, who provided the excellent illustrations for the technical sections of the book. Above all I am grateful to my dear Anna, who saw me through the direction of Mars to my hyleg and gave me the peace of mind to complete this work.

Symbols used in this book

Planets, points and aspects		Signs of the zodiac	
☉	Sun	♈	Aries
☽	Moon	♉	Taurus
☿	Mercury	♊	Gemini
♀	Venus	♋	Cancer
♂	Mars	♌	Leo
♃	Jupiter	♍	Virgo
♄	Saturn	♎	Libra
☊	Caput (north lunar node)	♏	Scorpio
☋	Cauda (south lunar node)	♐	Sagittarius
⊕	Part/Lot of Fortune	♑	Capricorn
♅	Uranus	♒	Aquarius
☍	opposition	♓	Pisces

Contents

Preface

Symbols used in this book

1.	The basics: what are primary directions?	1
2.	A brief history of primary directions	11
3.	The three-dimensional chart	33
4.	Directing planets	48
5.	Directing aspects	65
6.	The quest for precision	73
7.	Getting technical: more variables	82
8.	Modern innovations	88
9.	The hyleg and the length of life	106
10.	Primary directions and other predictive techniques	134
	Appendix I: Formulae for calculating primary directions	147
	Appendix II: Software offering primary directions	161
	Appendix III: The Egyptian terms and years of the planets	171
	Glossary	173
	Bibliography	181
	Index	187

1

The Basics: What are Primary Directions?

The technique known today as primary directions is one of the most ancient and renowned methods of astrological forecasting. It is also, as I hope to show in this book, one of the most powerful. From classical antiquity throughout the Middle Ages and Renaissance, and even into the twentieth century, all the great names of western astrology have worked with primary directions.[1] It was the predictive technique of Dorotheus and Ptolemy, of Māshā'allāh and Abū Ma'shar, of Regiomontanus and Placidus, of Morin de Villefranche and William Lilly. To understand the traditional astrologers, we must understand primary directions.

The primary motion

The word *primary* refers not only to the pre-eminence of the technique, but to the *primary motion* on which it is based. This is simply the daily rotation of the earth around its axis, appearing to us as the rotation of the sky – complete with planets, stars, and the signs of the zodiac – around our place of observation.[2] In approximately 24 hours not only the Sun, but every planet and zodiacal degree will rise in the east, culminate in the south (for an observer in the northern hemisphere), set in the west, and finally travel unseen across its lowest point in the north (the anti-culmination below the horizon) to the place where it will rise again.

A planet or point in the zodiac rising at the eastern horizon is said to be conjunct the ascendant. When culminating, it is similarly conjunct the midheaven or *medium caeli* (MC); when setting, conjunct the descendant; and when anti-culminating, conjunct the lower midheaven or *imum caeli* (IC). These four points or *angles* mark the cusps of the 1st, 10th, 7th and 4th houses, respectively, in all quadrant house systems. On its way between two angles, a planet or point will of course conjunct the intermediate house cusps as well; and it may also pass over places in the sky which minutes or hours earlier were occupied by other planets. We shall explore the mechanics of this more fully in Chapters 3 and 4.

Primary directions rest on this basic premise: that the actual motion of the heavens in the hours following birth, bringing the planets and other points to significant places in the natal chart, shows the unfolding of events in years to come; and that *each degree of such motion corresponds to approximately one year of life.*

As the earth turns on its axis, seemingly making the heavens turn around our vantage point, it completes a full circle of 360° in just under 24 hours, or 1440 minutes. One degree of primary motion therefore equals about 4 minutes of clock time (1440/360 = 4). This 1° motion is symbolically equated with one year, so that every hour after birth covers 15 years of life events. The directions formed to the natal chart within six hours of birth will then correspond to a full 90 years of life; and if a planet were to rise exactly two hours after a person's birth, we could expect whatever the planet signifies in the chart to manifest around 30 years of age in a way that affects the native's life, health, body and temperament (signified by the ascendant).

Interpreting primary directions

Like all predictive techniques, primary directions presuppose an understanding of the natal or radix (literally 'root') chart. The reading of the birth chart, which tells us the *What*, therefore precedes the timing of events, the *When*, just as a physician's diagnosis must precede his prognosis. The radix shows us the potential experiences of an entire lifetime all at once, often with confusing results as we see gain and loss, triumphs and setbacks jumbled together. We use directions and other predictive techniques to sort these influences into an ordered series of discrete events.

Because what is not promised in the radix cannot take place at any time, similar directions in dissimilar charts do not produce identical results. Nevertheless, an astrological 'family resemblance' may be found in all directions involving the same planet. This is because a planet always acts according to its own nature. The nature of a planet is the constant element in its effects, by which Mars signifies heat, conflict, suddenness or violence; and Venus, love, beauty, pleasure, or indulgence. The changing elements are the planet's relation to the houses of the chart (by location and rulership), which determines the areas of life it will affect; its dignities or debilities, which determine the quality and quantity of the results; and its relations with other planets (by conjunction and aspect), which determine both.[3]

To illustrate the points made so far, let us look at two natal charts where the Moon is about to rise.[4] In the first chart, the Moon is ruler of the 10th in the 1st, and as such promises success in career matters (unless afflicted, which it is not).

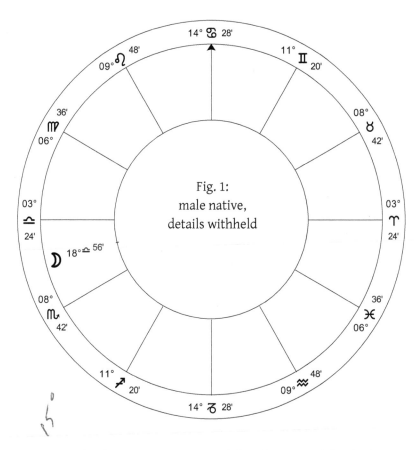

Fig. 1:
male native,
details withheld

Approximately 1h 57m, or 117 minutes, after the person's birth, the Moon rose over the eastern horizon. This corresponds to an event around 29.25 years of age, as every 4 minutes represent the rising of one degree (117/4 = 29.25). At the age of 29y 6m, the native gained an attractive academic position.

In the second chart, the Moon rules the 8th house, signifying suffering and misfortune. It also afflicts the ruler of the 7th house (marriage and love affairs) with a square aspect. The Moon rose over the horizon 1h 33m, or 93 minutes, after birth, corresponding to an event around 23.25 years of age. At 23y 6m, the native was plunged into a severe depression as a love relationship of six years' standing came to an end. (It is pertinent to note that when a planet is directed to the ascendant, its opposition is necessarily directed to the descendant, or 7th house cusp, at the same time. Directions of aspects will be discussed in detail in Chapter 5.)

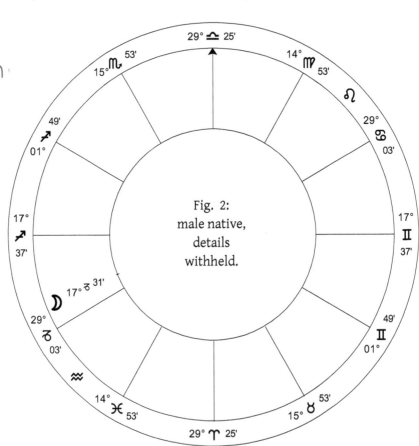

Fig. 2: male native, details withheld.

These two charts also illustrate the difference between degrees of ecliptical longitude (the 'zodiac degrees' shown in charts, with which students of astrology are most familiar) and degrees in the rotation of the earth (technically known as degrees of *right ascension*). In fig. 1, the Moon's longitude is less than 16° removed from that of the ascendant; yet the earth had turned 29° around its axis before the Moon rose. In fig. 2, the Moon is about 30° distant from the ascendant in the zodiac, but rose when the earth had turned only 23°. The reasons for this variation will be discussed in Chapter 3. For now, it will suffice to say that the rising times of the zodiacal signs differ, and that these differences become more marked the further one travels from the equator.

Significator and promissor

In both charts just discussed, the Moon is moving towards the horizon, which, as a great circle surrounding the place of observation, always remains fixed. This is the case in every primary direction: there is always one moving point and one which remains fixed.[5] Since the Middle Ages, astrologers have used the terms *promissor* (or, less correctly, *promittor*) and *significator* to differentiate between these two elements of a direction. Unfortunately, not all writers have employed these terms in the same way.

To older authors, a *significator* (sometimes also known as *moderator*) is a planet, angle or other chart point signifying a certain area of life, and considered the more passive element of a direction. Following Ptolemy, many classical authors have made use of only five significators, sometimes known as the 'hylegiacal points' (cf. Chapters 2 and 9): the ascendant, midheaven, Sun, Moon, and Part (or Lot) of Fortune. It was believed that all major events in life could be predicted from primary directions to these points. Not all astrologers agreed, however: 'Alī ibn Abī r-Rijāl, Jean-Baptiste Morin and William Lilly, to mention only a few, claimed all seven planets as significators.[6] Lilly's list is worth quoting here:

> First, the *Horoscope*, or Ascendant, we direct in every Nativity, for that it signifieth the Life and Body of man, his Complexion, the Affections and Manners of his Body and Minde [...]
> Secondly, we direct the ☽ in regard she signifies the Complexion of the Body, and its Intentions, the Natives Journeys, Peregrinations, his Matrimony, the state of his Wife, Women and neer Kinsfolkes.
> Thirdly, the Directions of the ☉ are made especially, concerning the Native's good or bad health, his Honour or Preferment publick or private, the favour of great Persons, the state of his Father, and his Estimation.
> Fourthly, *medium-cæli* we direct for Honour, Offices in the Common-

wealth, the friendship of Nobility, Kings and Magistrates, for the Magistery, Trade or Profession of the Native, for his Mother.

Fiftly, ⊕ being directed to the good or evill aspects of the *Fortunes* or *Infortunes* shewes the encrease or diminution of Riches [...]

Sixtly, you may direct ♄ to signifie your Ancestors, Inheritances, Buildings, Possessions, the Fruits of the earth; so also, Fears, Jealousies, Mistrusts, &c. according as ♄ is well or ill affected.

Seventhly, we direct ♃ for Glory, Renown, Riches, Children, Religion, Sobriety, &c.

Eightly, ♂ is directed for Animosity, Victory, War, Law-suits, and he shewes the estate of Brethren.

Ninthly, ♀ is directed for Matrimony, Love, Pleasure, rich Ornaments, Maids, Women, &c.

Tenthly, we direct ☿ for the Wit, Understanding, Trade, Industry, Negotiations, Journeys, our lesser Brethren, for Schollership, History, &c.

The Planets do signifie these things properly of themselves in Directions, in what Nativity soever they be, or in what part of Heaven; but accidentally, they have signification according to the nature of the Houses they are in, and are Lords of; by considering whereof, you shall finde the true intention of what is signified by the Direction.[7]

The *promissor*, on the other hand, is regarded as the active element, determining the nature of the event. The traditional promissors are mainly the seven planets and their aspects; some authors include the fixed stars in this group.[8] Typically, but not always (see below), the significator is either a fixed circle such as the horizon or meridian, or else *considered* as fixed in its natal position in the sky, while the promissor is carried towards it by the primary motion. Thus, in our examples, the fixed circle of the horizon or ascendant is the significator, while the moving Moon is the promissor.

In this context, however, it is important to be aware of a possible source of confusion. As the clockwise primary motion causes the signs of the zodiac to pass over the fixed place of the significator, that place appears to move anti-clockwise, that is, forwards through the signs. Classical authors, envisioning directions *from this point of view of the significator*, speak of directing a significator *to* a promissor (for example, 'the ascendant directed to the Moon'), although it is clear from their examples that they are in fact observing the promissor (the Moon) being carried by the movement of the celestial sphere towards a fixed significator (the horizon or ascendant).[9]

Direct and converse

In the context of determining the length of life (discussed in Chapter 9), Ptolemy distinguished between two types of directions. In the first type, a promissor is borne towards the significator with the primary motion from east to west as described above. As already noted, the zodiacal signs are carried clockwise across the significator, producing the impression that the significator is moving forward through the zodiac. Ptolemy therefore called this motion 'into the following signs'; later generations of astrologers referred to it as *right* or *direct* motion.

In the second type of direction, it is the significator which is carried clockwise towards a promissor with the same primary motion from east to west. As the significator may now be said to move backwards through the zodiac in order to reach a point in an earlier sign or degree, Ptolemy called this motion 'into the preceding signs'. Later authors knew it as *converse* motion.

In both cases, the astronomical motion of the celestial sphere from east to west is the same; but from the point of view of the significator, one direction is formed forwards along the zodiac, the other backwards. This distinction is related to the Hellenistic concept of aspects, where an aspect formed against the direction of the zodiacal signs (a dexter aspect) was known as *aktinobolia* (ἀκτινοβολία) or 'casting of rays' and perceived of as more powerful than one formed in the opposite direction (a sinister aspect). At no time was the celestial sphere imagined to move backwards, carrying planets from west to east.

The terms *direct* and *converse* retained the same meanings until the latter part of the 19th century, after which time they were radically altered (cf. Chapter 8). Directions in direct motion were the general norm, converse directions being used mainly for retrograde planets, so-called Arabic Parts, and certain life-span calculations. The two former conventions are of unknown origin, but present in medieval texts; the latter derives from Ptolemy (see Chapter 9).[10] In my own experience, I have found converse directions equally valid for all planets, whether retrograde or not.

SUMMARY

❖ Primary directions have been a major predictive technique of 'western' astrology for more than 1,500 years.

❖ The technique is based on the rotation of the earth around its axis (the *primary motion*), bringing planets and other chart points to new positions in the sky.

❖ Each degree of rotation, taking approximately 4 minutes of clock time, corresponds to one year of life.

❖ Every direction has two elements, one considered more passive as determining the area of life concerned (the *significator*) and the other considered more active as determining the nature of the event (the *promissor*).

❖ The promissor (generally a planet, aspect, or fixed star) being carried by the east-to-west primary motion to the natal place of the significator (generally a planet or angle) constitutes a *direct* or *right direction*. The significator being carried by the same motion to the place of the promissor constitutes a *converse direction*.

❖ The correct interpretation of a direction rests on the understanding of each planet's nature and signification in the natal chart, including its house position, rulership, dignities, and aspects.

REFERENCES

1. The term 'western' for a tradition largely upheld and developed by the Persians and Arabs has been rightly questioned. Indeed, the tradition as a whole is western only in relation to its easternmost cousin, the Indian tradition; nor have the two developed in isolation from one another. Primary directions, however, do not seem to have passed into India along with other parts of Hellenistic astrological teachings during the first two centuries of the common era.

2. This daily motion is called 'primary' because it was perceived by earlier astronomers as the rotation of the outermost sphere surrounding the earth, known as the *primum mobile* 'first movable'.

3. Some authors have tended to emphasize planetary nature at the expense of house rulership and position. For instance, Kühr 1936:348: 'Further it is advisable particularly to consider the nature of the promissors strongly in the interpretation. Nature not seldom proves superior to [house] determinations in directions *and under no circumstances proves false!*' My own experience, using a different zodiac and house system (see the Preface), has been that a planet's accidental determinations are as reliable as its nature.

4. Several example charts used in this book are anonymous, but all have well-documented birth times.

5. The two possible exceptions would be directions to intermediate house cusps in certain house systems (cf. the discussion in Chapter 4) and Placidean 'rapt parallels' (cf. Chapter 8).

6. See Abenragel 1551:161 (Haly Abenragel being the common Latinized name of ar-Rijāl, an 11th century author). Morin used the seven planets along with all twelve house cusps as significators, stating that Johann Schöner (15th – 16th century) had been of the same opinion; see Holden 1994:8.

7. Lilly 1659:653 f. A note in the margin reads: '*It's not usual to direct but the former five.*'

8. See, for instance, Lilly 1659:665 ff (drawing on medieval sources).

9. In the 11th century, al-Bīrūnī noted the same problem: 'It can be imagined from their terminology and their work that the progression [i.e., direction] is directed from the preceding (body) and ends at the following (body), but this is not the case. Its (real) meaning is

contradictory to that idea: it is the arrival of the following (body), by the primary motion (of the universe) to the place of the preceding (body).' (11th treatise of the *Masudic Canon*, unpublished translation by J. P. Hogendijk; additions in square brackets mine.)

10. Ar-Rijāl writes of these conventions (Abenragel 1551:158): 'Note that the direction (*athazir*) of the hyleg and planets is according to the order of the signs, commencing from the beginning of the sign and proceeding to its end, except among the Parts and retrograde planets, the direction of which is against the order of the signs: for it begins from the end of the signs and goes towards their beginning. The opinion of Ptolemy and his followers is that whenever the hyleg should be in the eighth house or the ninth, its direction is similarly against the order of the signs: which other sages do not allow, but direct it in the direct mode.' (Ptolemy does not in fact allow the hyleg to occupy the 8th house; see Chapter 9.)

2

A Brief History of Primary Directions

Before delving further into the technicalities of primary directions, it is useful to know something of their history. This chapter is not intended to be exhaustive, but merely to give an idea of the development and use of the technique over the centuries.

Hellenistic and Perso-Arabic astrology

The principles of primary directions are ancient, although the technique was not always known by that name. Its original inventors in Hellenistic Egypt naturally referred to it by a Greek word: *aphesis* (ἄφεσις) 'sending out, release'. Medieval authors writing in Arabic translated this as (*at*)-*tasyīr* 'letting run', which in its turn was Latinized as *athazir* or translated into Latin as *directio* in the sense of 'aiming at, sending in a straight line'. Only after the 17th century invention of so-called *secondary* directions – today generally known as *progressions* – did the qualifying word 'primary' become necessary for the earlier technique (see the section on Placidus below). Before that time, 'directions' meant primary directions.

Although surviving paraphrases of the Hellenistic astrologer Balbillus (d. c. 79 CE) suggest the use of directions for longevity calculations even in the 1st century BCE, our earliest worked example of the technique comes from Dorotheus of Sidon (fl. c. 75 CE), who wrote five books in verse on astrology known as *Carmen astrologicum* 'the song of astrology' or simply as the *Pentateuch* 'five volumes'.[1] Unfortunately, only fragments of these books have been preserved in the original Greek, and the passages relating to directions are not available except in an interpolated, second-hand Arabic translation dating from around 800 CE (based on a 4th-century Pahlavi version). One of the two example charts from this section can be dated to 381 CE, but the other most probably dates from Dorotheus' own time (fig. 3).[2]

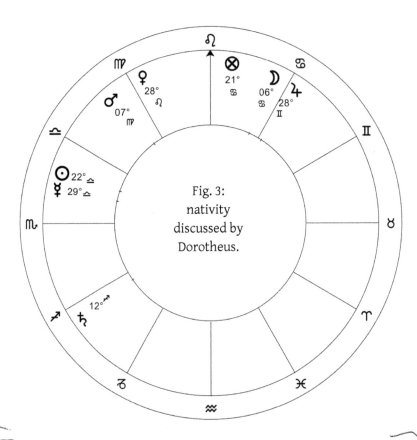

Fig. 3:
nativity
discussed by
Dorotheus.

Dorotheus takes the ascendant as the main significator of life (cf. Chapter 9), and proceeds to note the degrees of the zodiac passing over it by primary motion. In doing so, he pays attention both to the unequal divisions of the signs known as *horia* (ὅρια), 'bounds' or 'terms', and to the aspects of the planets.[3] Noting that 1° of the first terms of Scorpio remained to rise over the horizon at birth, terms both ruled and aspected by Mars, the author remarks:

So Mars takes over the governorship of the prorogation (i.e., direction) and ray (i.e., aspect). Until this degree in its prorogation and its ray ends without the ray of any [other] (planet), Mars indicates in this year injury from fire and disease. Even though Mars is in a good place, it is necessary that it indicate like this [...] Then the prorogation of the ascendant comes to the term of Venus till the eleventh degree. Because Mars has left and Venus has entered it is necessary to mix the power of these two together. Because of this the native will be blessed with love from his parents because both of these [planets] are in a good place, and moreover pain will reach him. Then till the nineteenth degree is the prorogation of Mercury, and in this period he will increase [his] learning and culture and the like.[4]

The terms of the planets, passing over the horizon one after the other, thus give rise to periods of several years, during which the natures of the planets are expected to manifest in a marked fashion. Dorotheus goes on to include the effects of aspects in his delineations:

Then the prorogation comes to Saturn while Venus casts [its] rays to the twenty-seventh degree of Scorpio from quartile (i.e., square), so that Saturn and Venus govern this prorogation together [...] Because of the place of Saturn his mother will die in this period, but he will acquire goods because Saturn indicates these, and he will marry a wife with dowry, and [a child] will be born to him who will live a short while and die in the third year; his enjoyment of women and children will be from Venus, but his lament and the death of his child will be from Saturn.[5]

Although most events are not timed even to the year of their occurrence, the predictions as such are concrete and fairly detailed. The predicted birth of a child that would die in its third year is suggestive, and probably relates to the aspect of Venus falling some 3° before the end of the terms of Saturn (and of the entire rising sign).[6] Dorotheus seems to regard Saturn, ruler of the terms, as setting the tone of the period, with the aspect of Venus to those terms giving less stable results.

Noting the rising of zodiacal degrees over the eastern horizon or ascendant appears to have been the earliest form of the direction technique. The arcs of direction were easily, if not always very correctly, approximated using tables of the times required for each zodiacal sign to rise over the horizon in a given *clime* or zone of geographical latitude. Soon, however, astrologers began to direct points to significators other than the ascendant; and many – perhaps not more astronomically astute than the average modern astrologer – happily continued to use zodiacal rising times to convert the distance between two points into time. The approximate number of degrees of the equator rising along with each sign was treated as a symbolic number of years associated with that sign, irrespective of whether or not it was actually rising in the chart under consideration.[7] Because a zodiacal sign requires different amounts of time to rise, set, culminate, or cross some intermediate point, such a procedure no longer corresponded to astronomical reality.[8]

Instances of this simplistic technique are found in several authors of
the late classical period, such as Vettius Valens (120 – c. 175 CE) and Paul of
Alexandria (fl. 378 CE).[9] The latter gives an example chart with Mars in 23°
Leo and the Sun in 15° Scorpio (fig. 4).

In order to direct the Sun to the square of Mars (located in 23° Scorpio),
Paul first assumes the local rising time of Scorpio to be 35 equatorial
degrees (140 minutes of clock time), corresponding to 35 years of life.
As the whole of Scorpio (30° in the zodiac) makes up 35 years, he then
takes each degree of Scorpio to represent 35/30 = 1 year 2 months. The 8°
between the Sun and the square of Mars thus represent 8 × 1y 2m = 9 years
4 months, at which time there would be mortal danger.[10] We thus see that
a zodiacal sign is assumed to rise at a uniform speed, which would then
increase or decrease abruptly as the next sign begins to rise. In reality, of
course, such is not the case.

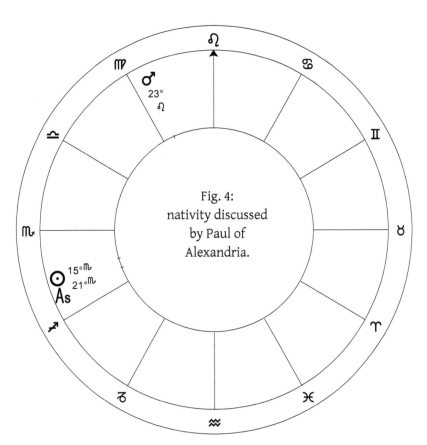

Fig. 4:
nativity discussed
by Paul of
Alexandria.

One author who objected to this procedure was Claudius Ptolemy (c. 100 – c. 178). The time of a direction, he wrote, should not 'be taken simply or off-hand, in accordance with the usual traditions' – that is, by merely noting the rising times of the signs – unless one is actually directing a promissor to the eastern horizon, or to a planet situated on it. If a direction is made to the upper or lower midheaven or to a planet on it, the time of the direction should be found by degrees of right ascension. And if a significator is located *between* the horizon and meridian, as is often the case, an intermediate method should be used to find out when the promissor arrives at a corresponding position: 'For a place is similar and the same if it has the same position in the same direction with reference both to the horizon and to the meridian.'[11] These ideas will be fully explored in Chapter 3.

While Ptolemy is our earliest source for this method, he does not claim to have invented it, stating merely that 'one method alone is available for him who is considering this subject in a natural manner [...] We shall therefore adopt [this] one method only'.[12] In fact, although most of his material is undoubtedly derivative, Ptolemy never names his sources. His one allusion to another author is to an unnamed 'ancient', sometimes interpreted as a reference to Petosiris, and appearing – not without significance – at the beginning of the chapter dealing with directions.[13]

Ptolemy himself was primarily a natural philosopher or 'scientist', and there is nothing in his brief astrological work, the *Tetrabiblos*, to indicate that he was a practising astrologer. Like many astrological authors of the modern era, he was concerned with providing natural explanations for the workings of astrology based on contemporary scientific theories, and with simplifying and streamlining existing astrological concepts in order to fit them into his theoretical framework. Ptolemy's teachings therefore deviate considerably from those of other Hellenistic authors, a fact which he does not attempt to deny:

> [W]e shall decline to present the ancient method of prediction, which brings into combination all or most of the stars, because it is manifold and well-nigh infinite, if one wishes to recount it with accuracy [...] and furthermore we shall omit it on account of the difficulty in using it and following it.[14]

Among the subjects which Ptolemy declined to discuss were, as noted by James Holden, most of the building-blocks of standard astrological interpretation both before and after his time, such as the effects of planets

...s and houses, their mutual aspects and rulerships. [15]

Ptolemy's two most important contributions to the development of astrology were his adoption of the tropical zodiac (not favoured by astrologers before his time) and the method of directions which he outlined.[16] Like other authors of his era, Ptolemy viewed directions first and foremost as a means of determining the length of a native's life. This determination of longevity formed the basis of all other predictions, and we shall examine it in some detail in Chapter 9. But directions could also be used to prognosticate other major events. Ptolemy describes his suggested method as follows:

> We shall apply the prorogation [i.e., direction] from the horoscope [i.e., ascendant] to events relating to the body and to journeys abroad; that from the Lot of Fortune to matters of property; that from the moon to affections of the soul and to marriage; that from the sun to dignities and glory; that from the mid-heaven to the other details of the conduct of life, such as actions, friendships, and the begetting of children.[17]

The number of significators was thus limited to five (often known as the *aphetic* or *hylegiacal* points; see Chapter 9). This model was to become standard procedure for many centuries, although dissenting voices were heard.

With the fall of the Western Roman Empire in the 5th century CE, knowledge of the Greek language and sciences, including astrology, dwindled and died in western Europe. In the east it was at least partly preserved, first in the Byzantine Empire and later by scholars of varying ethnicity and religion writing in Arabic. A major centre of such learning was the House of Wisdom (*Bayt al-Ḥikma*) in Baghdad, founded in the 8th century by Caliph al-Manṣūr (712 – 775), where Greek, Persian and Indian texts were translated and new works composed. Many of these Arabic texts have since been lost entirely, while others are available to us only in Latin translation.

The Perso-Arabic astrology which emerged over the next few centuries, including directions, was based on a mixture of Ptolemaic and mainstream Hellenistic techniques. In his *Three Books on Nativities*, 'Umar aṭ-Ṭabarī (better known by the Latinized versions of his name, Aomar or Omar Tiberiades; d. c. 815), speaks of two methods of directing. The first is by 'ascensions', which is to say the rising times of the signs. This practice, as discussed above, is that found in Vettius Valens. 'Umar ascribes it to

Dorotheus, saying that it is the one which 'nearly all of us who distribute rays [i.e., aspects] accept, and it is effective'. The second method is that of Ptolemy, who 'said that all rays should be assembled in a cusp, that is, in the point of the earth'.[18]

As is clear from 'Umar as well as later authors, directing the terms or bounds of the planets to the ascendant continued to be an important technique, dividing a native's life into planetary periods lasting several years.[19] The ruler of the terms, and thereby of the period, was known in Arabic as *(al)-jānbaḥtān* or *(al)-jānbaḥtār*, from a Persian word meaning 'dispenser of life' – itself a translation of the Greek *biodotēr* (βιοδοτήρ). This Perso-Arabic word was Latinized in medieval translations as *algerbuthar* (with many variants). A purely Arabic term for the term ruler was *al-qāsim*, translated into Latin as *divisor*.[20] The result of a period depended on the nature and placement of the divisor and of the planets configured with it, but also on any planets occupying or aspecting the terms themselves.

Directions by rising times seem also to have been favoured by Sahl bin Bishr (fl. first half of the 9th century).[21] A very concise paragraph in his work *On times* suggests some points of interest:

> And from the direction of the degree of the Ascendant or some one of the planets, to any degree, one year and a month and a day or an hour, in front or behind, up to some one of the planets, to its rays and theirs, and to the degrees of the signs and the Lots, is a time. And Māshā'allāh has already said before – and Abu 'Ali al-Khayyat (that is, his successor) – they have said, "for, direct the degrees in longitude and latitude, in front and behind."[22]

First, it appears that Sahl equates degrees not only with years, but with shorter units of time as well. This would probably be more useful in dealing with horary questions than with birth charts, unless it was meant for the prediction of death in infancy. Second, the phrase 'in front or behind [...] to its rays and theirs' suggests a free use of planets and their aspects ('rays') – the conventional promissors – as the fixed elements in directions. This relates to the discussion of direct and converse directions in Chapter 1.[23]

Sahl's reference to latitude is not clear: it may conceivably be a very early instance of directing the actual positions of the planets in the sky rather than their zodiacal degrees (cf. Chapter 4), but is perhaps more likely to refer to the consideration of latitude in the *interpretation* of directions. This, indeed, was standard practice: arcs of direction, and thereby the times of events, were calculated using zodiacal degrees rather than the actual bodies of the planets; but the effectiveness or otherwise of a direction depended on the latitude (if any) of the promissor. In general, a planet on the ecliptic was considered more effective than one with latitude; and if promissor and significator had latitude of opposite kinds – one north, the other south – the direction was considered weak. (Cf. Ptolemy's rules concerning lethal directions in Chapter 9.)

About a century later, al-Qabīsī ʿAbd al-ʿAzīz (better known as Alcabitius or Abdilaziz, with variants; d. 967) gave a detailed description of the Ptolemaic method of direction in his *Introduction to the Art of Judgments of the Stars,* which was to become a standard work of reference for many centuries.[24] Al-Qabīsī makes no mention of directions by mere rising times, nor does the Persian polymath al-Bīrūnī (973 – 1048), who calls the calculation of directions to significators located between the angles of the chart 'a long and difficult business'.[25]

The late Middle Ages and Renaissance

In the 12th century, the thin trickle of astrology which had been seeping into western European culture for some two hundred years grew suddenly into a swift stream. Arabic texts were translated into Latin, either directly or by way of the vernaculars, and soon original works were being composed in Latin. Among the more impressive of these was the voluminous *Liber Astronomiae* or *Book of Astronomy* by Guido Bonatti (c. 1207 – c. 1296). Despite the size of the work, however, Bonatti's treatment of directions is scant and largely based on ʿUmar. It thus comprises both the Dorothean and the Ptolemaic methods of direction, which Bonatti attempts to reconcile:

> Indeed ʿUmar said that Ptolemy worked by another method [than the method ascribed to Dorotheus], but, however, it was not contrary to this, even though it seemed different from it. Perhaps it seemed more difficult to some.[26]

The two methods are in fact irreconcilable; and as we have seen, Ptolemy had rejected the method of rising times outright. It is true, however, that Ptolemy's suggested method was more mathematically involved; and Bonatti, after a brief and not very clear account of it, refers his readers to al-Qabīsī for details.[27]

From antiquity, primary directions had been particularly associated with the prognostication of longevity. Medieval authors continued to develop and modify the rules connected with this procedure (discussed in

Chapter 9), but the methods of calculating directions remained essentially unchanged. Beginning in the Renaissance, we see a marked tendency to favour Ptolemy's longevity rules as well as his method of directions, apparent in such 14th – 16th century authors as Antonio de Montulmo, Johann Schöner, and Cardan.[28] One of the most influential figures of this time was undoubtedly Johann Müller (1436 – 1476), better known by the Latinized name Regiomontanus taken from his Bavarian home town Königsberg. His reinterpretation of Ptolemy would be adopted by most European astrologers over the next few centuries, and change their calculations of both houses and primary directions between planets (cf. Chapter 4).

A fervent adherent of the Regiomontanus system and reformer of astrology was Jean-Baptiste Morin of Villefranche (1583 – 1656), who sought to restore the intellectual position of astrology at a time when it was losing ground on the European Continent. Morin had made primary directions the cornerstone of his elaborate system of predictive techniques, which he detailed in his magnum opus, the voluminous *Astrologia Gallica*. He also refuted authors who attacked astrology in general and directions in particular. One of these was the humanist philosopher Pico della Mirandola (1463 – 1494), whose comprehensive objections Morin discusses at length. Making use of one of Pico's own rhetorical phrases, Morin concludes:

> Thus far, then, it has been evident how absurd, how false, and how inappropriate Pico's reasons against astrological directions are; the truth of which he himself experienced very bitterly, when, in the 33rd year of his age, immediately after he had written his twelve books against astrologers, he had to die from the direction of his Ascendant to the body of Mars in the 2nd, opposed to the Moon in the 8th, and square Saturn and [Mercury], as had been predicted to him by Lucio Bellantio, a physician of Siena, Antonio Syrigato of Florence, and Angelo de Catastini, a Carmelite [...][29]

The name more closely associated with primary directions than any other, however, is that of Morin's junior contemporary, Placido de Titi (1603 – 1668), generally known by the Latinized version of his first name, Placidus. According to his perhaps most famous statement, Placidus 'desired no other guides but Ptolemy and Reason'.[30] Ptolemy being a most incomplete guide for a practising astrologer, the proportion of Placidus' own reason in the resulting system was, for better or worse, correspondingly large. The

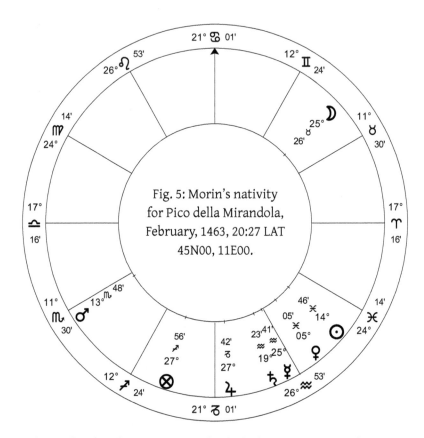

Fig. 5: Morin's nativity for Pico della Mirandola, February, 1463, 20:27 LAT 45N00, 11E00.

uses he made of Ptolemy's text speak of scholastic training and ingenuity, but would have greatly surprised its author.

Among the inventions for which Placidus tried to establish Ptolemaic authority were his *secondary directions* and *progressions*, both intended to supplement and support the main technique of (primary) directions:

> We call these motions the secondary directions, to distinguish them from the primary and principal; and we are of opinion, that Ptolemy, speaking of annual places, is to be understood of the places of those motions, and when of the menstrual [i.e., monthly], hints at the places of the progression.[31]

Today, secondary directions are generally known to astrologers as *secondary progressions* or simply *progressions*, while the 'progressions' of Placidus seem largely to have fallen into oblivion.[32] There is no mention of either technique in Ptolemy, who, in the place referred to by Placidus, was in fact writing about yearly and monthly *profections* – in modern terms, 'symbolic directions' (see Chapter 10). Like Morin, Placidus was determined to purge astrology of everything 'fictitious' or merely symbolical and establish it firmly on the basis of Aristotelian natural philosophy and physics; but unlike Morin, he chose to ascribe highly unlikely intentions to Ptolemy rather than criticizing him outright. Placidus also prided himself on using only the five Ptolemaic significators (ascendant, midheaven, Sun, Moon and Part of Fortune), and complained that it was 'the practice of several professors' to employ all the planets as significators.[33] We shall deal with his ideas in some detail in later chapters.

But Placidus was not to be honoured as a prophet in his own country. Despite having been thrice censored and approved by the Catholic Church, his *Physiomathematica*, originally published around 1650, was placed on the Index of forbidden books in 1687, a decision renewed in 1709. Instead, Placidean teachings eventually found a haven in Protestant England.

The glory days of English astrology came late, as interest in the subject was waning on the Continent. The era is epitomized by the figure of William Lilly (1602 – 1681), who, like most of his contemporaries, followed the Regiomontanus method of directions, as explained in his *Christian Astrology*. Lilly's two most well-known students were John Gadbury (1627 – 1704), who later turned against him and whom Lilly would describe as 'that monster of ingratitude my *quondam* taylor'; and Henry Coley (1633 – 1707), who proved more loyal and eventually became Lilly's adoptive son.[34] Both men published their own works on astrology including Regiomontanian primary directions, covering largely the same material (as did a score of other 17th-century writers), although Coley's *Key to the Whole Art of Astrology* goes somewhat further in explaining the basics of spherical trigonometry and the recently discovered method of logarithms.

In 1679, yet another English astrologer published yet another general introduction to astrology. The author was John Partridge (1644 – 1715), and the work was entitled ΜΙΚΡΟΠΑΝΑΣΤΡΩΝ *[Mikropanastrōn]: Or an Astrological Vade Mecum*, a small book promising to teach the reader as much as 'the great Volumes of Guido, Haly, or Origanus'. It also contained a laudatory epistle by 'John Gadbury, Student in the Syderal Science, unto the Readers of [...] my good Friend Mr. John Partridge' as well as a collection of Gadbury's own astrological aphorisms. Fourteen years later, Partridge published his *Opus Reformatum* ('reformed work'), in which he rejected the doctrines of the medieval astrologers in favour of Ptolemy and Placidus, although the latter is rarely mentioned by name.[35] More particularly, the book sets out to refute Gadbury, who is abused on nearly every page of the book, not only as an incompetent, ignorant and dishonest astrologer, but as a traitor and a turncoat. The background of this bitter attack lay in Gadbury's new-found Catholic sympathies during the religio-political struggle over the English throne towards the end of the 17th century.

Partridge's own sympathies lay with the Parliament and in particular with Oliver Cromwell, whose nativity and Placidean directions are discussed extensively in *Opus Reformatum*. He was also favourably disposed towards William Lilly, whose religious and political views (not to mention his long-standing feud with Gadbury) seem to have made up, in Partridge's eyes, for his clinging to erroneous astrological ideas. *Opus Reformatum* was soon followed by *Defectio Geniturarum*, in which Partridge criticized the analyses of nativities found in earlier writers, particularly on the subject of fatal directions. These writers included Argol and Morin but the main target was once again Gadbury (to whose *Collectio Geniturarum* Partridge's title alludes).

Partridge was by no means the only English astrologer of his day to take the Placidean teachings to heart. Others included Richard Kirby and John Bishop, who a few years before had published *The Marrow of Astrology* – an unacknowledged and somewhat abbreviated translation of Placidus' own work with very little original content added.[36] But there is little doubt that Partridge was the most instrumental in bringing about the Placidean revolution in England – and, by extension, in making Placidus the grandfather of modern western astrology.

From 1700 to the present

Following its unprecedented popularity in the 17th century, English astrology all but vanished in the 18th. The one name worth noting in connection with primary directions during this century is that of John Worsdale (1766 – 1826), whose major work first appeared in 1796 and was published posthumously by his son in a final enlarged edition in 1828. It bears the characteristic title *Celestial Philosophy or Genethliacal Astronomy, containing the only true method of calculating nativities, made plain and easy.* Few readers, whether of the 19th or the 21st century, would agree with the optimism of the last few words, although the work does repay study. Its introductory dedication, in verse, 'to the memory of the immortal Ptolemy', sets the tone:

Immortal Teacher of this Art divine,
Thy rules on record, most refulgent shine;
To thee alone we owe what we profess,
Though other Sages toil'd without success;
[...]
Yet all thy rules which infidels surprise,
Are daily proved in the boundless Skies,
Sages unborn, thy learning will adore,
Till Sun and Moon and Stars, shall shine no more.[37]

There is little poetry in the book as a whole, but the author's allegiance to Ptolemy as interpreted by Placidus is evident throughout, although the name of Placidus is never mentioned – no doubt due to Worsdale's frenzied anti-Catholic bias, which makes Partridge look positively tolerant. The style is terse and highly technical, except for occasional outbursts condemning 'Infidels, Deists, and Atheists' (along with baby-eating popish priests) as well as recent 'pirates [who] have dishonoured this predictive science by the fallacious innovations, and notorious prevarications which pollute their pages'. Apart from Partridge, who provides a Protestant source for Placidean techniques, Lilly is the only English astrologer to escape relatively unscathed.

Like Partridge, Worsdale was severe on those who dared deviate from Ptolemy, and he was proud of keeping to the 'Original Greek Quadripartite' (the Latin title of the *Tetrabiblos*) – adding in one place that 'with respect to the Quadripartites *lately* Published, we have no more *proofs* of their having been *originally* written by the *immortal* PTOLEMY, than we have of their [having] been composed by the *Roman Pontiff*'.[38] Nevertheless, both Partridge and Worsdale made full use of the innovations introduced by Placidus, such as minor and mundane aspects, which would have seemed strange indeed to Ptolemy. (See Chapter 9 for samples of Partridge's and Worsdale's work.)

Worsdale also introduced innovations of his own – most notably, an entirely new definition of the terms (or bounds) of the planets:

The old Tables which contain *certain Numbers* in the signs of the Zodiac, being the *supposed Planetary Terms*, are all *whimsical notions*, and void of Truth; the *true Terms* arise from clear demonstration, they may be discovered by Calculation in every Nativity, and those Calculations fully prove their use and power; the fact is, they are *those places* where the Benefics, and Malefics claim their greatest influence in the *Zodiacal*, and *Mundane Circles*, and are found by adjusting the difference, as the Stars approach to, or decline from the preceding Angle at Birth [...][39]

Unfortunately this is all the explanation he offers, leaving the reader ignorant of the precise method of performing the calculations to which he attaches such importance.

Judging from his work, Worsdale's main interest seems to have been in the prediction of death. All his example charts concern the correct method of finding the giver of life (the *hyleg*, cf. Chapter 9) and its lethal directions, sometimes with ill-concealed satisfaction at the fulfilment of dark forecasts made to disbelievers. Indeed, one historian has spoken of 'the pathological pleasure that Worsdale derived from acquainting clients, or others who had offended him, with the date they might expect to die'.[40]

The 19th century saw the beginnings both of the popularization of astrology in Britain and of its subsequent distortion. It was during this period that a simplified version of Placidus' system was confirmed as the standard of modern astrology by authors such as R. C. Smith (Raphael I, 1795 – 1832), R. J. Morrison (Zadkiel I, 1795 – 1874) and W. J. Simmonite (c. 1800 – c. 1860). Among the authors of this and the early 20th century, one particularly worth noting for his writings on primary directions is Alfred John Pearce (1840 – 1923), also known as Zadkiel II.[41]

Pearce was a fierce advocate of the technique, and of the mathematically rigorous, no-nonsense view of astrology which, to him, it embodied. Those astrologers who gave it up he censured as being 'too lazy' or 'imperfectly educated'; and in 1902, he declined an offer to join the newly founded Society for Astrological Research, saying that he could 'only unite with those who followed the Placidean method of *Primary Directions*'.[42] This short-lived society included, among others, Sepharial and Alan Leo, more of whom shortly.

Despite his claim to follow Placidus, Pearce deviated from Placidean teachings in several respects. He was among the first to redefine the concept of converse directions to mean directions against the primary motion (cf. the discussion of this concept in Chapter 8).[43] Pearce also denounced the 'old Arabian method' of secondary directions.[44] This was a false attribution, secondary directions being, as we have seen, a fairly recent invention of Placidus'; but blaming Arabic authors for whatever elements in astrology one did not approve of had been a favourite European pastime since the Renaissance.

Around the turn of the last century, Placidean doctrine, having been stripped of its scholastic-Aristotelic dress, was in the process of being – in the words of Wilhelm Knappich – 'shrouded in the shimmering magic cloak of Indian Theosophy' instead.[45] Pearce had no time for such ideas, which he regarded as 'superstitious nonsense' and 'nauseating'.[46] The younger generation of astrologers was less fastidious, however, and the two writers on directions of this era most well-known today were both practising Theosophists. They were W. R. Old, better known as Sepharial (1864 – 1929), and Alan Leo (originally W. F. Allen, 1860 – 1917).

There is no doubt that Sepharial – who eventually became disenchanted with Theosophy, and with Leo's 'esoteric' astrology – was the better astrologer of the two. Despite some idiosyncratic ideas and terminology, the calculations found in his books are generally correct. Leo, on the other hand, seems barely to have understood what he was doing (cf. the example chart in Chapter 8), and eventually abandoned the classical technique altogether. Holden observes:

> Leo was also responsible for a major shift in astrological predictive techniques. Prior to his appearance on the scene, primary directions had been the favorite tool of the astrologer. But primaries are bothersome to calculate [...] Leo's solution to the problem was to produce what he called "the progressed horoscope." This is a mixed bag of secondary directions and zodiacal primaries [...] His technique was soon adopted by most Western astrologers, since it was easier and quicker. Thereafter, the use of primary directions rapidly declined to a low level from which it has never recovered (despite the recent advent of computers to do the hard work).[47]

By the late 19th century, the renewed interest in astrology had spread to the Continent, often in conjunction with an interest in Theosophy and occultism generally. Morin's *Astrologia Gallica* was rediscovered and studied in France and Germany; but in general classical works were difficult to come by. Simplified textbooks were accepted as authoritative representations of traditional technique, speculation and invention serving to fill the inevitable lacunae. Among the few more technically astute European astrologers who continued to use primary directions in the 20th century, particular mention may be made of the German Erich Carl Kühr (1899 – 1951), whose *Berechnung der Ereigniszeiten* ('Calculation of the times of events') has become a modern classic. Kühr was greatly influenced by Morin, but preferred Placidean directions 'under the pole' (cf. Chapter 8) and Placidus houses to the Regiomontanus system.

After the Second World War, European astrology was dominated by English-language books, and the knowledge of primary directions continued to dwindle while new, mathematically simpler techniques multiplied. In the words of a British author writing two decades after the end of the war:

> Some practitioners use so-called Primary Directions, which require exacting mathematical calculations. These are not widely employed in this age of 'instant astrology'. In any case they are far too complicated for elderly ladies who dabble with horoscopes in suburban back parlours.[48]

With the revival of traditional astrology beginning during the last decade or so of the 20th century, however, and particularly with the increasing availability of ancient and medieval primary texts, interest in the technique has again begun to grow.

SUMMARY

❖ Directions were known in Greek as *aphesis* (ἄφεσις) 'sending out, release', in Arabic as *(at)-tasyīr* and in Latin as *athazir* or *directio*. The term 'primary directions' came into use only after Placidus invented the so-called *secondary* directions (now known as *secondary progressions*) in the 17th century.

❖ Directions may have been used as early as the 1st century BCE, but the earliest preserved example chart probably dates from the 1st century CE.

❖ The earliest form of directions was noting the rising of zodiacal degrees over the eastern horizon. Particular attention was given to the term ruler of these degrees, known in Greek as *biodotēr* (βιοδοτήρ) 'dispenser of life', and later as *al-jānbaḥtān* or *al-qāsim* in Arabic, *algerbuthar* or *divisor* in Latin.

❖ The arcs of direction were often approximated using tables of rising times for the zodiacal signs. When applied to distances between points not on the eastern horizon, these tables no longer corresponded to astronomical reality.

❖ In the 2nd century, Ptolemy proposed an astronomically correct procedure, which may also have been in use before his time. He further limited the significators used to the ascendant, midheaven, Sun, Moon, and Part of Fortune. Medieval Perso-Arabic authors give both techniques, but only the Ptolemaic model survived into the European Renaissance.

❖ In the 15th century, Regiomontanus proposed a new (and mistaken) interpretation of Ptolemy which won great support throughout Europe and gradually became the standard method of primary directions. It was the method used by Morin de Villefranche and William Lilly.

❖ In the 17th century, Placidus launched a return to the original Ptolemaic method, mixed with ideas of his own based on scholastic-Aristotelian natural philosophy. His system eventually caught on in England, where it was promoted by

John Partridge and John Worsdale, and (in simplified form) became the modern standard during the 19th century.

❖ During the late 19th and early 20th centuries, British astrology was radically simplified and increasingly connected with Theosophy and occultism. From this time, the use of primary directions rapidly declined both in Britain and on the European Continent, to which the astrological revival had spread. Only since the last decade of the 20th century has this trend begun to reverse.

REFERENCES

1. The two extant Balbillus charts, of which the earlier can be dated to 72 BCE, are discussed in Neugebauer & Van Hoesen 1959:76 ff; cf. Chapter 9.
2. Pingree 1976:xv dates this second chart to 20 October, 281 CE; but I agree with Holden 1996:34 that a date of 2 October, 44 CE, conforms better to the chart.
3. There are several versions of the terms. Dorotheus used the so-called Egyptian terms; see Appendix III.
4. Pingree 1976:243 f. Additions in round brackets are mine.
5. Pingree 1976:244. Additions in round brackets are mine.
6. The 'twenty-seventh degree' is in the text, although the accompanying chart shows Venus in the 28th degree of Leo.
7. Robert Hand's comment (in Schmidt 1995:40) that in this method 'two points were considered joined together if they were made capable of rising together' is perhaps rather misleading. The method consisted in roughly converting the zodiacal distance between two points into degrees of oblique ascension (cf. Chapter 3). The two points in question would never actually rise together.
8. The celestial mechanics involved in directions will be more fully discussed in Chapter 3. For now it will suffice to say that the daily path of a planet across the sky passes the meridian (midheaven) at right angles, where it is therefore measured in *right ascension*; but its

movement across the horizon is slanted and therefore measured in *oblique ascension.*

9. Paul's text begins (Greenbaum 2001:1) with the assertion that he has revised an earlier work to include the 'more useful' directional method of Ptolemy (detailed below); but the method he actually puts forth is the common one rejected by Ptolemy.

10. Greenbaum 2001:71.

11. Robbins 1940:286–291.

12. Robbins 1940:286–293. Additions in square brackets are mine.

13. Robbins 1940:270 f.

14. Robbins 1940:227.

15. Holden 2008d:xii ff. Holden describes the *Tetrabiblos* – with some asperity but, in my opinion, correctly – as 'a small book on astrology [... which] has exercised an influence on Western Astrology out of all proportion to its intrinsic merit [... Ptolemy] was obviously unwilling to devote the time and effort necessary to do the subject justice', and further notes that '[t]he ancient method that he found so complicated and difficult is in fact quite similar to that used in Horary Astrology, which has been transmitted to us from the Greeks more or less intact only because Ptolemy chose to ignore it'.

16. The Hellenistic astrology which reached India in the early centuries CE was pre-Ptolemaic, and Indian astrology has therefore preserved the sidereal zodiac. As late as the 9th century, some Perso-Arabic astrologers (such as Māshāʾallāh and Abū Maʿshar) still worked with sidereal positions, possibly taken from Indian tables; but with the increasing influence of the Ptolemaic tables, the European tradition in existence since the later part of the Middle Ages has until quite recently been exclusively tropical.

    Two points are worth noting with regard to Ptolemy's zodiacal reform: First, that the tropical definition of the zodiac was purely an academic issue to Ptolemy and his contemporaries, as it in fact coincided with the sidereal definition in the early centuries CE. Ptolemy relied heavily on Hipparchus (c. 190 – c. 120 BCE), who was an astronomer but not an astrologer, and adopted his tropical definition of the zodiac, no doubt because it appeared more exact and 'scientific' than the sidereal zodiac traditionally used by astrologers; but this made little difference in practice. Only centuries later did the precession of the equinoxes cause the two zodiacs to grow sufficiently apart for the distinction to matter greatly; and astrologers are therefore far better equipped today than in Ptolemy's time to determine which zodiac gives better results. Second, that Ptolemy's 'scientific' arguments for the tropical zodiac, being based on seasons and climate conditions in the northern hemisphere, are in fact invalid unless one is prepared to reverse zodiac rulerships south of the equator (and perhaps abolish them altogether in the tropical zone, where there are no seasons in Ptolemy's sense).

For a discussion on the sidereal zodiac used in early Hellenistic astrology and later, see Holden 1996:11 ff *et passim*. Also cf. Chapter 3 below for a discussion on astronomical coordinate systems.

17. Robbins 1940:449. Additions in square brackets are mine.

18. Hand 1997:18 ff. Additions in square brackets are mine. Hand remarks that it 'is not at all clear what is meant by the assembling of all of the rays onto the point of the earth'. The phrasing probably alludes to *Tetrabiblos* 1.24, where Ptolemy states that the rays of the planets 'always fall and similarly converge from every direction upon the same point, that is, the centre of the earth' (Robbins 1940:115). In the present context, I believe 'Umar refers to the fact that a 'ray' or line extending from the radical place of a planet to the earth will intersect the semi-arcs of other planets proportionally (cf. Chapter 4).

19. See, for instance, Hand 1997:40–49.

20. Kunitzsch 1977:38.

21. Sahl writes: 'Therefore, direct this [sc. significator] just as you direct the *hīlāj* to the conjunction of the malefics and their aspects, giving a year to every degree, *by the ascensions of that city.*' (Dykes 2008:229, emphasis mine.)

22. Dykes 2008:224 f. Holden 2008c:189 seems correct in rendering the Latin word *consutor* as 'The Tailor' (a translation of the Arabic name al-Khayyāt) rather than, as Dykes, 'his successor'. More importantly, however, Holden translates: '[Māshā'allāh and al-Khayyāt] have [both] said *not* to direct the degree in longitude and latitude forward or backward' (emphasis mine). This negation is based on the abbreviation .n., occurring in the 1493 edition used by Holden and interpreted as *non* 'not' (personal communication with the author). A more likely interpretation of .n. is *enim* 'indeed, certainly', which is in fact the word occurring in the corresponding place in Zahel 1519:129r. Here Dykes

has the better translation.

23. *Pace* Dykes 2008:224, n. 18, Sahl's statement does not suggest 'converse' directions in the present-day sense, calculated against the primary motion; cf. Chapter 8.

24. Al-Qabīsī's work was translated into Latin in the 12th century. For his teaching on directions, see Burnett et al. 2004:121 ff (English translation along with editions of the Arabic and Latin texts).

25. Wright [1933] 2003:382 f. Al-Bīrūnī had also adopted Ptolemy's tropical definition of the zodiac, and seems to have been ignorant of the fact that another definition had ever existed; thus he criticized Indian astrologers for having 'no knowledge of the motion of the fixed stars towards the east' (Sachau [1888] 2002: 493).

26. Dykes 2007:1145. Additions in square brackets are mine.

27. Dykes 2007:1415.

28. Almost nothing is known of Montulmo (fl. late 14th century) except that he was a 'doctor of medicine and the arts' and wrote a work entitled *On the Judgment of Nativities* (Hand 1995a). Johann Schöner (1477 – 1547) wrote *Three Books on the Judgments of Nativities* (the first book being available in English translation, Hand 2001) as well as *Opusculum astrologicum* ('A small work on astrology', Hand 1996). Gerolamo Cardano, 1501 – 1576, known in English as Cardan, was an extremely prolific author and polymath whose books reflect several changes and developments in his ideas over the years. To my knowledge, except for a brief collection of aphorisms, none of his surviving astrological works has been translated into modern languages.

29. Holden 1994:144 f. The printed translation mistakenly has 'Mars' in the place of 'Mercury'. As Holden points out, Pico actually died in his 32nd year, not the 33rd; the mistake may have been caused by rivalling calendaric systems. A five-minute change in the time of birth would adjust the directions by about one year.

30. Cooper [1814] 2004:47.

31. Cooper [1814] 2004:25; additions in square brackets mine.

32. The Placidean 'progressions' equate one synodic month (based on the exact relationship between the Sun and Moon) with one year of life. The technique was used by English followers of Placidus in the 18th – 20th centuries and is briefly described in Pearce [1911] 2006:239 f. In the mid-twentieth century, German astrologer E. H. Troinski proposed

a similar technique (based on the tropical, rather than synodic, month), naming it 'tertiary directions'.

33. Cooper [1814] 2004:126.

34. Lilly's comment about Gadbury is found in Lilly [1715] 1822:86.

35. Cooper [1814] 2004:iv notes: 'It was from this book [by Placidus] that Mr. Partridge took all the best of the matter which he inserted in his Opus Reformatum and Defectio Geniturarum, though he very rarely acknowledged the obligation.'

36. *The Marrow of Astrology* was reissued only a year after its first publication, this time under the sole name of John Bishop and with a preface by none other than Henry Coley, who does name Placidus as the originator of the method taught, if not of large portions of the text itself. Coley mentions *'Dr. Wright, Thomas Moor Esq. Mr. Worral* and [...] *Mr. John Partridge'* as other contemporary English adherents of Placidus, and feels that their endeavours 'ought to be encouraged, and assisted, as Aiming at Truth it self, and not rejected and rediculed, (as some are too forward to do)'.

37. Worsdale 1828:xix f.

38. Worsdale 1828:154.

39. Worsdale 1828:141.

40. Howe 1968:27.

41. Morrison, the first 'Zadkiel' on the English astrological scene, was succeeded after his death by one R. V. Sparkes, who died only a year later, so that Pearce was really the third editor of *Zadkiel's Almanac* (see Curry 1992:110). Morrison and Pearce, however, were the more well-known of the three.

42. See Pearce [1911] 2006:183; Curry 1992:138.

43. For examples, see Pearce [1911] 2006:182 ff.

44. Pearce [1911] 2006:183.

45. Knappich 1935. The amount of genuinely Indian ideas actually contained in the Theosophical mélange is debatable.

46. Quoted in Curry 1992:111.

47. Holden 1996:195.

48. Howe 1968:419.

3

The Three-Dimensional Chart

We all know what an astrological chart looks like, but what does it really depict? In this chapter we shall examine the astronomical coordinate systems underlying the horoscope, some of which may seem more familiar than others. It is necessary to understand these fundamental mechanics of planetary motion in order to appreciate the workings of primary directions.

The wheel-shaped chart is an attempt to capture in two dimensions the three-dimensional reality of the heavens surrounding us at a given point in time and space. It may in fact be understood as the image of a sphere – known as the *celestial sphere* – seen from an imaginary point outside it.

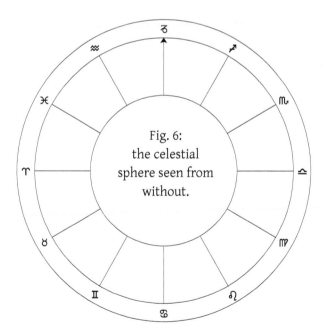

Fig. 6:
the celestial
sphere seen from
without.

Within this sphere are several imaginary circles (in two dimensions) known as *great circles*, which we use to orient ourselves and to define the position of objects we observe in the sky. A great circle is so called because its dimensions are the greatest possible within the sphere, meaning that its centre is also the centre of the sphere. Any great circle therefore divides the sphere in half. The five great circles dealt with in this chapter are: the horizon, the meridian, the prime vertical, the equator, and the ecliptic.

The horizon

Imagine that the place where you are sitting or standing were free of any obstacles to vision – walls, houses, trees, hills – so that you could see all the way to the horizon in every direction. You would then find yourself at the centre of a vast circle. This is the great circle of the horizon, which can be extended infinitely into space. In the wheel chart, we see it only as a line – the horizontal line dividing the chart into a visible and an invisible half – as if we were looking at the thin edge of a disc. The left side of this line shows the eastern half of the horizon, the right side shows the western half.

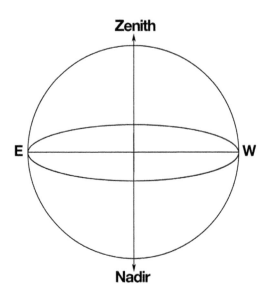

Fig. 7: the plane of the horizon.

The position of a planet or point in the sky is measured in two ways with reference to the horizon: by degrees along the circle, known as *azimuth,* and by degrees above and below the circle, known as *altitude.* A planet exactly on the horizon has 0° altitude.

Properly speaking, the horizon just described – having for its centre a point on the surface of the earth – is known as the *topocentric horizon.* For reasons of mathematical simplicity, most calculations employed in astrology make use of the *geocentric horizon,* which is a circle exactly parallel to the topocentric horizon but centred around the core of the earth, some 6,000 kilometres beneath our feet. Although this distance may seem great to us, in astronomical terms it is so small as to be negligible. (One exception to this – the lunar parallax – will be discussed in Chapter 7.) The important point is that both these circles are at right angles to the *axis* of the place of observation (the birth place, for a natal horoscope), which is an imaginary line passing through the centre of the earth and through the observer to the points exactly overhead and below: the *zenith* and *nadir.*

It should be emphasized that this geocentric horizon passing through the

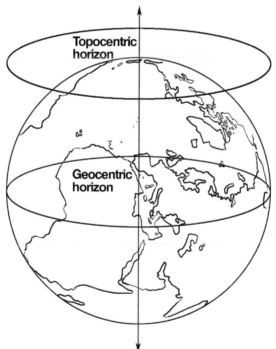

Fig. 8: the topocentric and geocentric horizons.

centre of the earth has nothing to do with the equator. Many of us have been conditioned, by maps and illustrations of the earth, to think of north as 'up' and, consequently, of the equator as the only line across the middle of the world. But unless we live on the North Pole, the point above our heads ('up') will *not* be north, and the plane on which we stand – or any plane parallel to it, no matter how far below us – will be tilted with respect to the equator. (See further on the equator below.)

The meridian and the prime vertical

As we have just seen, the circle of the horizon is divided into an eastern and a western half. The vertical line dividing them in the wheel chart is really another circle viewed edgeways. This upright circle extends from the southernmost point of the horizon through the zenith of the observer, the North Pole of the earth's axis, the northernmost point of the horizon, the nadir or point directly below the observer, the South Pole of the earth's axis, and back to the south point of the horizon. Thus, if you stand facing due south, the circle will pass through the points straight ahead of and behind you, as well as directly above and below.

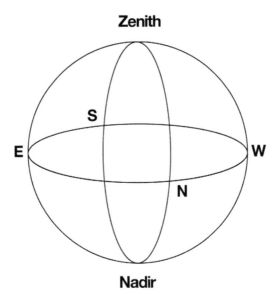

Fig. 9: the circle of the meridian intersecting the horizon due south and north.

This great circle is known as the *meridian* (from Latin *meridies* 'midday'), as it marks the position of the Sun at local noon, when the Sun reaches its highest point. The same is true of any planet or point: all reach their culmination when conjunct the meridian above the horizon, and are at their lowest point (anti-culmination) when conjunct the meridian below the horizon. The point of culmination is known as the midheaven or *medium caeli* (MC). This should not be confused with the zenith or point directly overhead: only near the tropics does a planet ever pass exactly above the place of observation.

Yet another great circle passing through the zenith and nadir is the *prime vertical,* which intersects the east and west point of the horizon, at right angles to the meridian. It is not much used in astrology, except in the Campanus house system.[1] Neither the meridian nor the prime vertical is normally used to define the celestial position of a planet.

The equator

The two great circles of the horizon and meridian always remain fixed with respect to the place of observation, the horizon marking the places where planets and signs of the zodiac rise and set, the meridian the places where they culminate and anti-culminate. This daily motion, as we know, is caused by the rotation of the earth around its axis, but appears to us as the rotation of the celestial sphere around our vantage point. The great circle marking the direction of this rotation is the *celestial equator*.

The celestial equator may be seen as the projection into space of the earthly or *terrestrial* equator. Just as the horizon is a circle perpendicular to the line between the points directly above and below the observer (the zenith and nadir), so the equator is a circle perpendicular to the line between the earth's North and South Poles – its axis – around which it rotates. This means that the position of the celestial equator in the sky depends on our location on earth. For an observer at 0° geographical latitude – for instance, in Central Africa or South America – the celestial equator will pass exactly overhead, at right angles to the horizon (and therefore coinciding with the prime vertical). For an observer at the North Pole, on the other hand, the celestial equator will coincide with the horizon. At other locations in the northern hemisphere, the equator is a circle intersecting the horizon at the points due east and west, and culminating somewhere to the south, where it intersects the meridian at a point determined by the geographical latitude.

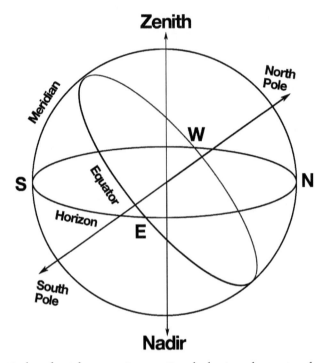

Fig. 10: the celestial equator intersecting the horizon due east and west.

As its name suggests, the celestial equator divides the horizon equally. On the two days of the year when the Sun is exactly on the equator (cf. below), it will spend the same amount of time above and below the horizon, making day and night of equal duration. These days are the vernal and autumnal equinoxes, around 20 March and 22 September.

The position of a planet or point in the sky is measured in two ways with reference to the equator: by degrees along the circle, known as degrees of *right ascension*, and by degrees north and south of the circle, known as *declination*. A planet exactly on the equator has 0° declination. As the celestial equator turns in the sky, it crosses the meridian at right angles at a uniform speed of just under 4 minutes per degree, completing a full circle of 360° in 23h 56m. The passing of one such degree of right ascension over the meridian is equated in primary directions with approximately one year of life. (The equation of degrees with years will be examined more fully in Chapter 6.)

A phrase often mentioned together with right ascension is *oblique ascension*. The oblique ascension of a planet or zodiacal degree is simply the point on the celestial equator (that is, the degree of right ascension) which would rise along with it over the eastern part of the horizon. It is so called because the horizon, unlike the meridian, does not intersect the equator at right angles, but obliquely. Similarly, the *oblique descension* of a planet is the point on the celestial equator which would set along with it at the western horizon.

The ecliptic and the zodiac

We now come to the coordinate system most familiar to astrologers in general. The yearly orbit of the earth around the Sun appears to us as the movement of the Sun through the fixed constellations. This motion, of the Sun and other planets, is called the *secondary motion* and takes place from west to east, against the direction of the primary motion (except when planets occasionally turn retrograde for some time).

The movement of the Sun by secondary motion takes place along a great circle known as the *ecliptic* (so called because eclipses occur when the Moon conjuncts or opposes the Sun in this circle). The Moon and other visible planets are always found within a belt of some 9° to either side of the ecliptic. This belt is the *zodiac*. The distance of a planet north or south of the ecliptic is called *latitude*. By definition, the Sun is always exactly on the ecliptic, at 0° latitude.

A planet's position along the ecliptic is known as *longitude*. In astrology, longitude is normally expressed as degrees from 0° to 30° within the zodiacal signs, which are equal twelfths of the ecliptic. Originally, the starting-point of the first sign (0° Aries) was defined with reference to the fixed constellations (the *sidereal* zodiac). During late antiquity and the early Middle Ages, however, the definition advocated by Ptolemy gradually gained territory, and 0° Aries was increasingly defined as the vernal equinoctial point, where the ecliptic intersects the equator (the *tropical* zodiac).[2]

Had the earth's axis been perpendicular to the plane of its orbit around the Sun, we should have seen the Sun constantly on the equator; in other words, the equator would have coincided with the ecliptic. As it is, the earth's axis is inclined to its orbit at a current angle of 23°26'. This means that the ecliptic appears to us as a lopsided circle, inclined to the equator at the same angle (known as the *obliquity of the ecliptic*). Thus, while the equator always intersects the horizon exactly at the east and west points,

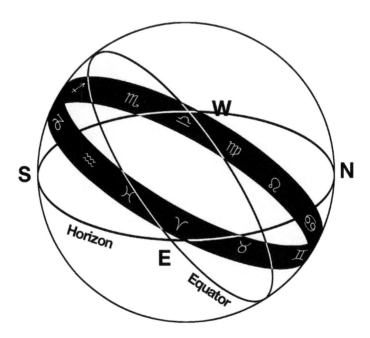

Fig. 11: the ecliptic, surrounded by the band of the zodiac, inclined to the equator.

the ecliptic will typically appear askew – its rising point somewhere to the north-east and its setting point to the south-west; or, conversely, its rising point to the south-east and its setting point to the north-west. The only exception is when, twice a day, the equinoctial points (where the ecliptic and equator intersect) are found exactly on the horizon so that the ecliptic rises due east and sets due west.

The obliquity of the ecliptic is also related to the positions of the polar circles on earth and the phenomenon of *circumpolarity*, where an ecliptical degree does not rise or set. As the geographical latitude of an observer begins to exceed 66°34′, so does the distance of the observer's zenith from the celestial equator. Consequently, the maximum declination of the horizon, which is at right angles (90°) to the zenith-nadir line, grows less than 23°26′ (90° - 66°34′ = 23°26′), which is the maximum declination of the ecliptic (its obliquity from the equator). This means that one part of the ecliptic will have a declination which is constantly above the horizon: it never sets, but only circles the place of observation by its diurnal motion. The opposite part of the ecliptic will have a declination constantly below the horizon, so that it never rises. This is what causes the phenomenon of midnight sun in extreme northern regions, when the Sun occupies circumpolar degrees in the summertime – and, conversely, midday darkness in winter.

It is a fact well known to most astrologers that house systems either break down or have to be applied rather differently than usual at such extreme geographical latitudes. The same is true of primary directions. The traditional methods, as explained in this book, were developed far from the polar circles, and work as long as there are risings, settings and culminations to be observed. Quite possibly, similar sets of astronomically-based techniques could be discovered for locations near the North Pole; but that is a challenge for northern astrologers, and a subject for another book.

Plotting a planet

Of the five great circles just discussed – the horizon, meridian, prime vertical, celestial equator, and ecliptic – three are commonly used in describing the position of a planet. These are the *horizon, equator,* and *ecliptic*. With regard to each circle, the planet can be plotted both in terms of position *along* the circle and of position *above or below* the circle.

Let us look again at the chart from fig. 1. The position of the Moon can be defined in the following ways:

❖ With respect to degrees *along the ecliptic*, the Moon is at 18°56′ Libra, or 198°56′ from the starting-point of the circle (0° Aries). This is the Moon's *longitude*, shown in the chart.

❖ With respect to degrees *north or south of the ecliptic*, the Moon is south of it by 4°03′. This is the Moon's *latitude*, which is *not* visible from the chart. Southern latitude is often written as a negative number: -4°03′. Having latitude, the Moon is not located exactly on its degree of the ecliptic; rather, a line drawn from the centre of the Moon at right angles to the circle of the ecliptic will fall in 18°56′ Libra.

❖ With respect to degrees *along the horizon*, the Moon is 102°29′ distant from the north point (the point where the meridian intersects the horizon in the north). This is the Moon's *azimuth*, which tells us that the Moon is somewhat to the south-east (being more than 90° removed from the north point, and hence beyond the point due east). The degree

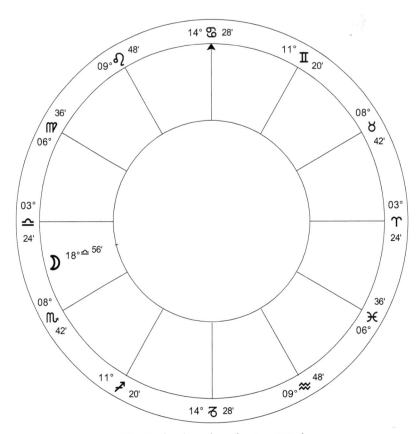

Fig. 12: the chart from fig. 1 revisited.

of azimuth is not visible from the chart, which only tells us that the Moon is in the eastern half of the circle of the horizon (to the left of the meridian line).

❖ With respect to degrees *above or below the horizon*, the Moon is below the circle with an *altitude* of -15°00'. In the wheel chart, the ☽ symbol is correctly shown below the horizontal line. It should be noted, however, that the chart shows not the actual position of the Moon, but that of its ecliptical degree. When a planet near the ascendant or descendant has latitude, its symbol may therefore be shown on the 'wrong' side of the chart's horizontal line. Again, as the Moon is not exactly on the horizon, its azimuth represents the position of a straight line drawn from the Moon's centre to the circle of the horizon.

❖ With respect to degrees *along the equator*, the Moon is 218°30′ distant from the vernal equinoctial point (the point where the equator intersects the ecliptic in the east). This is the Moon's *right ascension*, which is not visible from the chart. A rough idea can be had, however, from the fact that the vernal equinoctial point marks 0° Aries in the *tropical* zodiac.

❖ With respect to degrees *north or south of the equator*, the Moon is south of it, with a *declination* of -19°22′. This is not visible from the chart either, although a rough idea may be had from the fact that half the ecliptic (in the tropical zodiac, from 0° Aries to 0° Libra) is always north of the equator, the other half south of it. As before, the fact that the Moon is not actually on the equator means that its right ascension represents the position of a straight line drawn from the Moon's centre to the equatorial circle.

The two-dimensional chart thus gives us only an approximate idea of a planet's location in space. Good-quality astrological software, however, provides the above information in tabular format.

The diurnal circle and its semi-arcs

As we have just seen, due to the obliquity of the ecliptic, the degrees of the zodiacal signs rise and set at different points along the horizon (that is, at different azimuths). Each degree therefore traces its own unique arc across the sky, rising somewhere in the eastern half of the horizon, culminating as it joins the meridian in the south (for an observer in the northern hemisphere), and setting somewhere in the western half of the horizon. This arc is called the *diurnal arc* of the degree. It is worth noting that a planet other than the Sun may be in its diurnal arc even during nighttime (when the Sun is below the horizon) .

Naturally, the diurnal arc is complemented by a *nocturnal arc*, which is the arc traced by the same zodiacal degree in its journey below the horizon – from its setting point, across its anti-culmination at the lower meridian, and back to its rising point. The full circle of a degree, comprising both its diurnal and nocturnal arc, is called its *diurnal circle*. As the diurnal motion is caused by the daily rotation of the earth around its axis, all diurnal circles are parallel to the great circle of the celestial equator.

The rising and setting points of any zodiacal degree will always be equidistant from the meridian. A point rising 60° east of the meridian will therefore set 60° west of it, thus spending the greater part of its diurnal circle below the horizon. The diurnal and nocturnal arcs of a zodiacal degree will nearly always be of unequal length, the proportions varying according to the geographical latitude of the point of observation. Only the degrees on the equinoctial points, rising due east and setting due west, will divide their diurnal circles equally.

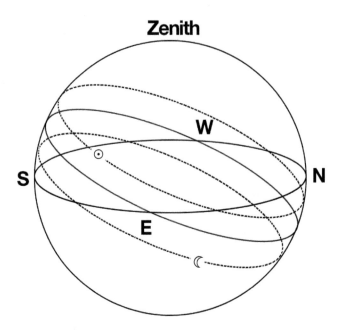

Fig. 13: the diurnal circles of the Sun and Moon are both parallel to the equator and do not touch.

Another way of explaining the same thing is to say that the meridian divides every diurnal arc – and, similarly, every nocturnal arc – into two equal semi-arcs. We can thus divide the diurnal circle of any point in the zodiac into four phases or semi-arcs:

❖ the diurnal semi-arc from the rising point (ascendant) to the culminating point (midheaven, MC);

❖ the diurnal semi-arc from the culminating point (MC) to the setting point (descendant);

❖ the nocturnal semi-arc from the setting point (descendant) to the anti-culminating point (lower midheaven, IC);

❖ the nocturnal semi-arc from the anti-culminating point (IC) to the rising point (ascendant).

What has just been said of the diurnal circles of the zodiacal degrees applies to the actual bodies of the planets in the sky as well: each planet will, by the rotation of the earth, trace its own unique circle across the sky, parallel to the equator – most often somewhat to the north or south of its zodiacal degree. This is because the planets, excepting the Sun, are rarely found exactly on the ecliptic, but rather have some latitude north or south of it.

In the next chapter, we shall build on this understanding of the diurnal circle, its arcs and semi-arcs, to describe the actual mechanics of primary directions and how they relate to real events in a person's life.

SUMMARY

❖ The astrological chart is a two-dimensional representation of the three-dimensional celestial sphere, the centre of which is our place of observation.

❖ Within the celestial sphere are several great circles, each of which divides the sphere into two equal parts. The most important great circles are the horizon, meridian, equator and ecliptic.

❖ The horizon is the great circle surrounding the place of observation, perpendicular to the line between zenith and nadir. Degrees along it are called azimuth; degrees above and below it, altitude. Planets and zodiacal degrees rise and set at the horizon.

❖ The meridian is the great circle passing through zenith and nadir and intersecting the horizon due south and north. Planets and zodiacal degrees culminate and anti-culminate at the meridian.

❖ The celestial equator is the great circle perpendicular to the earth's axis, marking the direction of the rotation of the earth. Its position in the sky depends on our location on earth, but it always rises and sets due east and west. Degrees along it are called right ascension; degrees north and south of it, declination.

❖ The ecliptic is the great circle describing the Sun's apparent motion during a year (secondary motion), and is currently inclined to the equator by 23°26'. Its rising and setting points on the horizon therefore vacillate over the course of a day. Degrees along it are called longitude; degrees north and south of it, latitude. The zodiac is a belt some 9° to either side of the ecliptic.

❖ Every planet and point in the chart has its unique diurnal circle, parallel to the equator and passing through the planet's points of rising, culmination, setting and anti-culmination.

❖ A diurnal circle is divided into a diurnal arc above the horizon and a nocturnal arc below the horizon, typically of unequal extension. Each arc is divided equally into two semi-arcs east and west of the meridian.

REFERENCES

1. Campanus (Latinized name of Giovanni Campano, 1233 – 1296) propounded, but did not invent, the house system named after him. It was known, two centuries earlier, to al-Bīrūnī, who favoured it over what he called 'the well-known method' (the standard medieval house system, nowadays known as Alcabitius) and 'the method of the ancients' (now known as the Porphyry system). See North 1986:32 f.
2. See Chapter 2, note 16, for a discussion of the tropical and sidereal zodiacs.

4

Directing Planets

Primary directions can be divided broadly into two groups: those in which a planet or point is directed to the *angles* of the chart – in o ther words, to the circles of the horizon or meridian – and those in which it is directed to the *place of another planet* or point.

Directions of the first kind are by far the simplest, and astrologers are unanimous in their views on how to calculate them. There can be no dispute about the distance of a planet or other point from the horizon and meridian, or about the time at which it rises or culminates at a given location on earth. (Other factors, discussed below and in Chapters 6–7, may still cause some differences in the timing of directions to the angles.)

Directions of the second kind are more problematic. This is because each planet or point, as discussed in the previous chapter, has its own unique diurnal circle, by which it will traverse the sky. Therefore, a planet will typically not reach the exact point in the sky previously held by another planet. Rather, we observe the movement of a planet to that position in its own diurnal circle which most closely corresponds to the position held at birth by another planet in *its* diurnal circle – and there is more than one way of defining 'corresponding most closely'.

Directions to angles

In Chapter 1, we saw two examples of directions to the ascendant. A planet – in both example charts, the Moon – rose at the horizon some time after birth, bringing about the manifestation in the natives' lives of whatever the Moon signified in the respective birth chart.

It is important to note that, for our purposes, the whole eastern half of the horizon is equated with the ascendant. It does not matter if a planet or zodiacal degree does not rise at the precise spot where our natal ascendant degree rose. In fact, we already know from the preceding chapter that it will not: the degrees of the ecliptic all have their own individual places of rising and setting. My natal ascendant degree (could I have seen it) may well have risen by this rock over here, and the Sun three hours later by that tree over there, but the sunrise still represents a direction of the Sun to my ascendant – bringing into my life whatever the Sun signifies in my birth chart – around the age of 45. (Three hours, or 180 minutes, corresponding to approximately 45° in the daily rotation of the earth, or degrees of right ascension.)

In the same way, the whole western half of the horizon is equated with the descendant; the upper half of the meridian, with the MC; and the lower half of the meridian, with the IC.

Example: the fame of River Phoenix

Let us look at a direction to the midheaven in the chart of actor River Phoenix. The Sun is very strongly placed in the 10th house, in its domicile (Leo), applying by sextile to Jupiter in the 1st.[1] As such, the Sun clearly

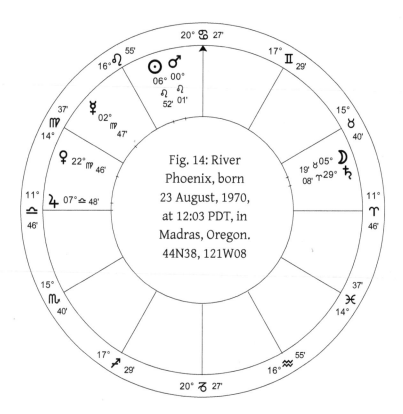

Fig. 14: River Phoenix, born 23 August, 1970, at 12:03 PDT, in Madras, Oregon. 44N38, 121W08

presages fame and honours; and a natural time to expect this rise to fame would be when the Sun is directed to its culmination, the MC.

Phoenix was born at 12:03 summer time, meaning that there was still about an hour left before true noon, that is, before the local culmination of the Sun – to be precise, 64 minutes of clock time. As the earth turns 1° in approximately 4 minutes, 64 minutes correspond to 16° of right ascension or 16 years of life. At age 16, Phoenix made his great career breakthrough with the film *Stand By Me*.

Unhappily, only seven years/degrees after this early and fortunate direction to the MC, Phoenix's ascendant was afflicted by the opposition of Saturn, immediately followed by the square of Mars. These were extremely dangerous directions and, with certain others, proved too malignant for him to survive. Phoenix died on 31 October, 1993.[2] (The direction of aspects will be discussed in Chapter 5, and the determination of life-span in Chapter 9.)

In the world or in the zodiac?

In directing the Sun, as we just did, there is no question of latitude, as the Sun by definition is always on the ecliptic with 0° latitude. With the other planets, however, we typically have a choice between directing the actual body of the planet as seen in the sky, or its longitude in the ecliptic (its zodiacal degree). The former is called a direction *in mundo* 'in the world', or a *mundane* direction. The latter is a direction *in zodiaco* 'in the zodiac', or a *zodiacal* direction. Whether for reasons of mathematical simplicity or from more philosophical considerations, directions in the zodiac are by far the older method. Only in the 15th century did directions *in mundo* come into general use.

In the older literature, directing a planet *in mundo* is sometimes called a direction *cum latitudine* 'with latitude'. When directing one planet to the conjunction of another, the two terms are interchangeable. When directing aspects, however, they are not: a zodiacal *aspect with latitude* is not the same as a *mundane aspect*. The methods of directing zodiacal aspects will be discussed in Chapter 5, mundane aspects in Chapter 8.

Depending on how much latitude the planet has, and in which part of the zodiac it is, the difference in timing between a mundane and a zodiacal direction may amount to several years. My personal experience has been that in charts with precise and well-corroborated birth times, the actual times of a planet's rising, setting, culmination and anti-culmination – that is to say, its *mundane* conjunctions with the angles – are the most effective; but the zodiacal conjunctions often produce an effect as well.[3]

Example: a double-edged planet
To illustrate the difference between a mundane and a zodiacal conjunction with the ascendant, see the following chart with Mars in the 1st house as ruler of the 10th (the midheaven).

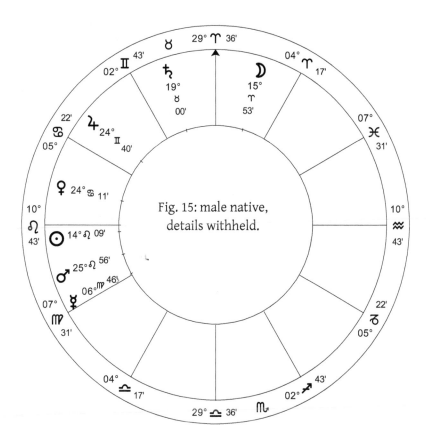

Fig. 15: male native, details withheld.

The position of Mars indicates professional success, the more so as Mars is a nocturnal planet in a nocturnal chart and receives a sextile aspect from Jupiter in the 11th. When Mars reaches the ascendant, a career advancement may therefore be expected. At the same time, however, Mars as a natural malefic is prone to harm the body and health, signified by the ascendant.

The longitude of Mars is 25°56′ of Leo. This point in the ecliptic reached the horizon 92 minutes after birth, corresponding to 23 years of age. However, as Mars has a latitude of 0°55′ north of the ecliptic, the planet itself will rise a little earlier than its ecliptical degree – about 3½ minutes earlier, corresponding to nearly a year in primary directions. This means that while the *zodiacal* direction of Mars to the ascendant is completed around the age of 23 years, the *mundane* direction of Mars to the ascendant is completed a month or two after age 22.

Do these directions correspond to real life events? Around the age of 23½ years, the native suffered a serious attack of glandular fever, resulting in prolonged hospitalization and a break in his university studies. A little more than a year later, he had received his degree and an attractive professional position. Both events agree with the natal promise of Mars. They are, however, somewhat too late to match the directions closely. This suggests that the recorded birth time may be a little too late, although an actual rectification of a birth time should never rest on as little as one or two events. Adjusting the given time by 4 – 5 minutes would make the events under consideration fall very neatly into place.

Being time-sensitive, directions to angles are the most useful for rectification work when the exact time of birth is in question; but this does not mean that all major events in life have their corresponding direction to the horizon or meridian. Some modern authors on primary directions have been of the opinion that directions to the angles are the most powerful, or even the only ones worth considering. This is neither a traditional view nor, in my experience, a correct one. The frequency of such directions will also vary greatly depending on the rising sign and the geographical latitude of the birth place. If we are not content to ascribe an event to any angular direction happening to coincide with it, but rather wish to see every planet working in accordance with its own nature and significations in the chart, then we must understand how to direct planets not only to the angles, but to each other.

Planet to planet: the semi-arc method

Imagine that you are standing out of doors in the small hours of a spring morning, a few days before the New Moon, somewhere in the northern hemisphere. As you watch the eastern horizon, you see the crescent Moon rising somewhat to the south-east. You watch it gradually climbing upwards and southward.

As the Moon ascends, dawn is approaching. Suddenly you see the golden disc of the Sun on the horizon, this time a little to the north-east. The pale Moon is still visible, and as you trace the arcs of the two luminaries across the sky during the day, you observe them culminating – first the Moon and then, some time later, the Sun. You notice that the Sun reaches higher in the heaven than the Moon. As afternoon turns to evening, the Moon sets a little to the south-west, and after a while the Sun too sinks below the horizon slightly to the north-west.

We see that the diurnal arc of the Sun never touches that of the Moon, but continues parallel to it. In this example, the Sun's diurnal arc is the longer one, as it rises and sets further from the meridian. But although the Sun never reaches the exact position where the Moon was at any given time – for instance, at nine o'clock in the morning – it does reach a point in its own arc *proportional* to that position. If we assume that, at nine o'clock, the Moon had completed 70% of its journey from rising to culminating – its diurnal *semi-arc* – then the Sun will reach a corresponding or proportional position after completing 70% of its own semi-arc. When it does, the Sun is said to be conjunct the nine o'clock position of the Moon. This is the *proportional semi-arc method* of directing originally propounded by Ptolemy and used throughout the Middle Ages.

Example: Mars attacks
The following chart will illustrate the principle. Mercury, ruler of the 1st house, is closely conjunct a fallen Mars, ruler of the 6th. This is an indication of frequent illnesses of a martian nature: acute, inflammatory, requiring surgery. Mercury, being the faster planet, is applying to Mars by secondary motion; but by primary motion it is Mars that will, not long after birth, reach a position corresponding to that of Mercury in the natal chart.

Like directions to angles, interplanetary directions too can be calculated either *in zodiaco* or *in mundo*. Although trigonometrical formulae for this purpose are given in Appendix I, it is possible to calculate the direction of Mars to the conjunction of Mercury in the zodiac without them, using a simple method which is easy to replicate – especially with astrological software that includes chart animation – and which illustrates the underlying idea of the proportional semi-arc method.

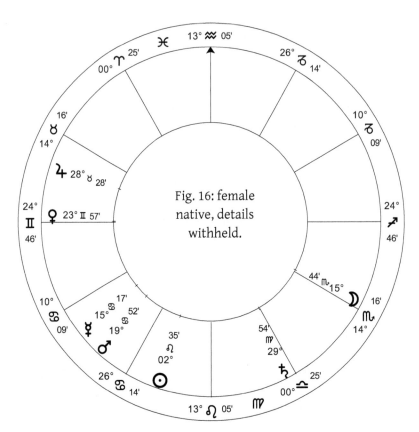

Fig. 16: female native, details withheld.

Mercury has a longitude of 15°17' Cancer and is between its points of anti-culmination (IC) and rising (ascendant). The following times, using 24-hour notation, have been rounded to the nearest minute. For times past midnight, we must occasionally add 24 hours.

a) 15°17' Cancer anti-culminates at: 23:10
b) 15°17' Cancer rises at: 03:01

The difference between these two times is the nocturnal semi-arc of Mercury in the zodiac, expressed in time (every 4 minutes roughly corresponding to 1° of right ascension).

c) Nocturnal semi-arc of Mercury: (03:01 + 24:00) - 23:10 =
                                           03:51 = 231 min.

Next, we find out how much of this semi-arc Mercury had traversed at birth.

d) Time of birth: 00:58

e) Elapsed time of Mercury's semi-arc at birth: (00:58 + 24:00) - 23:10 =
                                                   01:48 = 108 min.

f) Elapsed part of Mercury's semi-arc at birth: 108/231 (appr. 46.75%)

We see that Mercury had completed about 46.75% of its nocturnal semi-arc at the time of the person's birth. Now we need to find out how long after birth Mars would reach the corresponding point (46.75% or, more precisely, 108/231) in its own nocturnal semi-arc. Mars has a longitude of 19°52′ Cancer.

g) 19°52′ Cancer anti-culminates at: 23:28

h) 19°52′ Cancer rises at: 03:30

As above, the difference between these times is the nocturnal semi-arc of Mars expressed in time.

i) Nocturnal semi-arc of Mars: (03:30 + 24:00) - 23:28 =
                                                   04:02 = 242 min.

We now seek the point in this semi-arc corresponding to the position of Mercury above (f), and the time at which Mars will reach this point.

j) Corresponding point of Mars's semi-arc: 108/231 × 242 min. =
                                                   113 min.

k) Time of Mars reaching corresponding point: 23:28 + (113 min = 01:53)
                                                   = 01:21

Finally, we calculate how much time will have elapsed between birth and the time of Mars reaching the corresponding point.

l) Time of birth: 00:58

m) Elapsed time after birth: 01:21 - 00:58 = 00:23

Some 23 minutes after birth, Mars thus reached a point in its semi-arc corresponding to the position held by Mercury in its own semi-arc at birth. We now convert this time into degrees of right ascension by the approximate formula of 4 minutes = 1°, which gives us 23/4 = 5.75°. This is the *arc of direction* for Mars to the conjunction of Mercury in the zodiac. (More exact calculation gives an arc of direction of 5.83°.) Equating each degree with a year of life, we therefore see that the direction was completed not long before the native's 6th birthday. At the age of 6y 4m, the native was rushed to hospital with acute appendicitis and immediately operated on.

To calculate the corresponding *mundane* direction, we can substitute the anti-culmination and rising times of the actual planets for those of their zodiacal degrees and calculate as above. In the chart under discussion, the direction of Mars to the conjunction of Mercury *in mundo* has an arc of 5.26°, making a difference in time of approximately half a year. In this case, therefore, we see that the zodiacal direction is closer to the actual time of the corresponding major event. (See Chapter 6 for a detailed discussion of timing issues.)

An important note on house systems

In the 17th century, Placidus advocated a system of calculating houses based on the proportional semi-arc method of primary directions just discussed.[4] Two centuries earlier, Regiomontanus had similarly advocated a method of calculating directions based on the system of house division which bears his name – the circle-of-position method dealt with below.[5]

Regiomontanus and Placidus both seem to have felt it necessary, or at least more elegant, to direct planets and divide houses by the same method. This has led to the widespread misunderstanding that primary directions are a function of one's chosen house system. As is obvious from the history of astrology, however, they are not. In the 2nd century, Ptolemy, our oldest explicit source for the proportional semi-arc method of directions, apparently used equal houses. Throughout the Middle Ages, the same Ptolemaic directions were used together with several house systems – most commonly, Alcabitius.[6] There is no compelling reason (except perhaps a personal inclination towards minimalism) to suit one's method of primary directions to a particular system of house division or vice versa.

Regrettably, modern authors on primary directions have sometimes perpetuated the misunderstanding, even using directions as a cudgel with which to beat undesirable house systems.[7] They have also added to the confusion by inventing methods of directing which were never used historically, such as an 'Alcabitius' method based on the derivation of Alcabitius house cusps. The directional system actually explained in some detail by al-Qabīsī (Alcabitius) himself in the 10th century was of course the Ptolemaic semi-arc method.[8] Even more regrettably, unsuspecting software authors have implemented these modern misconceptions in their programmes.

Planet to planet: the circle-of-position method

For some 1,300 years after Ptolemy, the proportional semi-arc method remained virtually unchallenged. In the 15th century, however, Regiomontanus (1436 – 1476) claimed to have understood Ptolemy's real intentions with regard both to house division and to directions.[9] This belief, though earnestly held, was false; nevertheless, the 'rational method' proposed by Regiomontanus soon gained a following, no doubt partly due to the availability of his published tables. In the 17th century it was used by both Jean-Baptiste Morin and William Lilly. The latter wrote:

> The whole Art of Directions is copiously handled by *Regiomontanus* [...] but most exquisitely by [his follower] *Argolus* [...] At this day we use no method in Directions but *Argolus*, which is generally approved of in all parts of *Europe* as most rational.[10]

The Regiomontanus system rests on a brief passage in the *Tetrabiblos*, in which Ptolemy defines his understanding of 'similar places' in the arcs of different planets:

> For a place is similar and the same if it has the same position in the same direction with reference both to the horizon and to the meridian. This is most nearly true of those which lie upon one of those semicircles which are described through the sections of the meridian and the horizon, each of which at the same position makes nearly the same temporal hour.[11]

The operative word here is *nearly*: no circle or semicircle can connect all the points which at a given moment in time share the same relation to both the horizon and the meridian. Nevertheless, Regiomontanus' combined system of houses and directions is based on the idea of such circles. The great circles of the horizon and meridian are taken as the house circles (or cusps) of the 1st/7th and 10th/4th house axes, respectively. The meridian intersects the horizon at the north and south points, and the remaining house circles too are made to converge at these two points. Each intermediate house circle – in order of the primary motion, the 12th/6th, 11th/5th, and, following the meridian, the 9th/3rd and 8th/2nd houses – is positioned so as to divide the celestial equator into equal segments of 30° of right ascension.

To calculate a primary direction between two planets, a similar circle is drawn, passing through the body of a planet and again intersecting the horizon at the north and south points. This is called a *circle of position*. In this way the position of a planet – in itself a mere point – is converted into a great circle or artificial 'horizon', which every other planet must at some time or other cross during its own journey across the sky (in its diurnal circle). The *time* between birth and the moment at which planet A reaches the circle of position of planet B (or, put differently, the *distance* in right

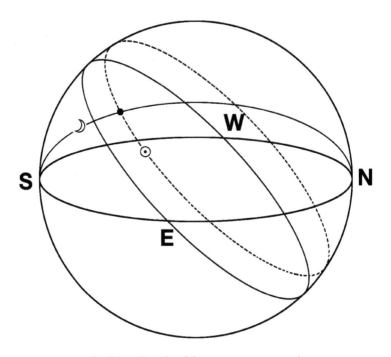

Fig. 17: the diurnal circle of the Sun intersecting the Moon's circle of position.

ascension between planet A and the intersection of its diurnal circle with the circle of position of planet B) is the arc of direction between the two planets.

Looking again at the chart in figure 16, a circle of position passing through the body of Mercury would intersect the diurnal circle of Mars at a point 5.47° distant (in right ascension) from Mars's own position. In other words, it would take Mars just under 22 minutes to reach the intersection point with Mercury's circle of position.

This direction is a mundane one, and not very far from the corresponding mundane semi-arc direction (5.47° and 5.26°, respectively). Such is not always the case, however: directions between the same two points by the semi-arc method and by circles of position may differ by several degrees, changing the timing of an event by years.

It is of course entirely possible to direct zodiacal degrees by circles of position as well; but Regiomontanus and his followers preferred to use the mundane positions of the planets and even assigned latitude to the aspects, using methods which will be discussed in the following chapter. The Regiomontanian arc of direction *in zodiaco* for our example chart would be 6.53°.

Directions to intermediate house cusps

On its way between two angles, a planet will necessarily cross the cusps of the intermediate houses. As the positions of the house circles (or, in the case of Placidus houses, curves) vary from one house system to another, so do the times of the planets' directions to them. Directions to intermediate house cusps are not mentioned by the earliest writers on the technique, and only sparsely by later authors.[12]

As we have just seen, Regiomontanus house cusps are circles intersecting the horizon (and meridian) at its north and south points, and directions to cusps are calculated exactly like directions between planets above. The same method holds for Campanus house cusps, which only differ from the Regiomontanus variety in that they divide the prime vertical equally rather than the celestial equator.

Planetary directions to Placidus cusps are altogether different, as these are not really house circles but rather curves, based on the rising and culmination times of each individual point. Each planet's diurnal circle therefore has its own set of 'built-in' house cusps, so that a planet that has traversed one third of its path from rising to culminating is considered to be conjunct the 12th house cusp; after two thirds, it is conjunct the 11th cusp; and so forth.

The Alcabitius system, used for many charts in this book, poses its own challenges. Alcabitius cusps are house circles dividing the equator at right angles and converging at the North and South Poles. The circle of the first house is therefore not the horizon itself, but rather a circle intersecting the horizon obliquely at the actual ascendant degree – that is, at the point where the ecliptic crosses the eastern half of the horizon. As the ascendant moves back and forth across the east point in the course of a day – now a little to the south, now a little to the north – the intermediate house circles will move with it. When a planet reaches the point in its diurnal arc intersected at birth by a house circle, the house circle will therefore no longer be in the same position. We thus face the question of whether to use the natal or the 'real-time' house circle. At present I do not know of any traditional sources pointing in either direction. My own experience in the field, though very limited, seems to suggest that directions to 'real-time' Alcabitius cusps may have some merit.[13]

SUMMARY

❖ All astrologers agree on how to direct planets to the horizon (ascendant/descendant) and to the meridian (MC/IC).

❖ Before the 15th century, only the ecliptical longitudes of the planets were typically directed. This is known as direction in the zodiac (*in zodiaco*), or without latitude.

❖ For the past 500 years, many astrologers have used directions of the actual bodies of the planets. This is known as direction in the world (*in mundo*), or with latitude.

❖ Directions to the angles are more sensitive to changes in birth time than directions between two planets, and therefore more suitable for rectification work.

❖ The Ptolemaic method for directing one planet or ecliptical point to another is to bring the moving point to a place in its semi-arc proportional to the place occupied by the fixed point in its own semi-arc at birth. This was the method in general use before the 15th century.

❖ Regiomontanus introduced another method based on circles of positions passing through the body of the fixed point (as well as the north and south points of the horizon) and intersecting the diurnal circle of the moving point, thus giving the arc of direction.

❖ Directions to intermediate house cusps are rarely mentioned in older astrological literature. The arc of a planet's direction to any cusp will depend on the house system used.

❖ It is not logically necessary to use the same mathematical methods for primary directions as for house division, and astrologers prior to the 15th century generally did not do so.

REFERENCES

1. Jupiter had risen above the horizon, but was still in the 1st house by traditional criteria, being in the rising sign and conjunct the cusp of the ascendant within 4°. Jupiter, a diurnal planet, is actually more powerful for being above the horizon in a daytime chart, making it *in sect* (cf. Chapter 9). For the diurnal and angular Sun to be favourably configured with this diurnal and angular benefic is highly fortunate. (Conversely, Jupiter on the ascendant is greatly benefited by being in sect and favourably aspected by the Sun. Phoenix was well-known for his strong moral stance on issues like animal rights and the environment.)

2. The cause of death was an overdose of heroin and cocaine. This is also reflected in the birth chart, where Venus as ruler of the 8th house is the main significator of death and occupies the 12th house in its fall, an evil position. In *The Judgments of Nativities*, Abū ʿAlī al-Khayyāṭ (9th century) states that if Venus as significator of death is impeded, 'it signifies death from sexual license or poisoned medicines' (Holden 2008d:85).

3. Even Morin, a staunch advocate of mundane directions, admits (if somewhat unwillingly) that such is the case. His views on the matter are worth quoting (Holden 1994:42 f): '[T]he ecliptic is the course or line of march most efficacious for [planetary] influence [...] Therefore, it is no wonder that after the point of the sign in which the true place of the Moon falls beyond the ecliptic, the point of its longitude in the ecliptic is more strongly determined to the nature of the Moon than the rest [...] But if that point on the ecliptic possesses the lunar virtue on account of the true place of the Moon beyond the ecliptic, it follows that the true place itself is of still greater virtue.' Morin goes on to say that an effect begun by a zodiacal direction may last until the time of the corresponding mundane direction or vice versa, and that one should consider the revolutions (in modern terminology, the solar return charts) for the years of both directions, as a direction will take effect only when the revolution agrees (cf. Chapter 10).

4. Placidus' model of house division had in fact been discovered earlier – it was known to 12th century astrologer Abraham ibn Ezra, who favoured it – but had not found wide support. See North 1986:20 ff.

5. The Regiomontanus house system is also known as *modus rationalis*, the 'rational method'. It was not, as is sometimes erroneously stated,

invented by ibn Ezra (cf. the previous note); but it was known before the time of Regiomontanus, and may have originated with al-Jayyānī (989 – 1079). See North 1986:33 ff.

6. The Alcabitius house system was named after 10th century astrologer al-Qabīṣī, but dates back at least to the early 5th century, when it was used by Rhetorius the Egyptian. See North 1986:4 ff, Neugebauer & Van Hoesen 1959:138 f.

7. Instances may be found throughout Makransky 1992 and Plantiko 1996: 'What relates the problem of houses to primary directions is the concept of *mundane position*, which is employed in the calculation of houses as well as directions. There are different concepts of mundane position, which lead to different systems of houses and of directions.' (Plantiko 1996:81) '[I]n fact every house system implies its own definition of what is meant by the term "conjunction," and every house system gives rise to its own unique method of computing primary directions.' (Makransky 1992:132)

8. See Burnett et al. 2004:121 ff. The fabricated 'Alcabitius system' of directions is found in Makransky 1992:67, among many similar inventions by the author.

9. The method advocated by Regiomontanus had actually been described four centuries earlier by al-Bīrūnī, who also advocated directions *in mundo*: 'Thus, if (the preceding body) is between these fundamental semicircles [of the horizon and meridian], it is necessary that their computation is by the ascensions of the circle passing through the preceding (body) and the two poles of the prime vertical, or by their descensions [...] if we intend [...] (to deal with) the case where the planet is at a distance of a (non-zero) latitude from the ecliptic, then it is necessary to consider the preceding body by itself, regardless of its ecliptical degree.' (11th treatise of the *Masudic Canon*, unpublished translation by J. P. Hogendijk; additions in square brackets mine.) Whether these ideas were in fact transmitted to Regiomontanus from some Arabic source is not known.

10. Lilly 1659:651; additions in square brackets mine.

11. Robbins 1940:290 f.

12. One medieval author to use intermediate cusps in directions was ar-Rijāl, as in this example (Abenragel 1551:160): '[There was] another nativity, the sixth house of which was in twenty-two degrees of Aries,

and its hyleg the first degree of Pisces, and Mars in opposition to the hyleg, and Venus similarly aspected the hyleg; and when the direction of the hyleg arrived at the degree of the sixth house, the native's slaves killed him [...]' Ar-Rijāl's method, however, was not to direct the planets to the cusps, but rather the zodiacal degrees on the natal cusps to the planets; cf. Chapter 8. For the concept of hyleg, see Chapter 9.

13. It may be noted that in the Alcabitius system, a planet directed to the horizon will not be conjunct the natal 1st house circle, but rather a new, 'real-time' 1st house circle (having a different azimuth). It would therefore seem inconsistent to use natal house circles for the intermediate houses.

5

Directing Aspects

In the last chapter we learned a new way (or rather, two new ways) of understanding the concept of *conjunction* – not by the secondary motion of two planets through the zodiac, but by primary motion along their own diurnal circles. In this chapter, we shall add *aspects* to conjunctions. There is little new arithmetic involved in directing aspects, although it may require some mental readjustment, and raise some new questions along the way.

Zodiacal aspects without latitude

To the inventors of primary directions, as well as to many generations of astrologers following them, an aspect was essentially a relationship between *signs of the zodiac*. Signs distant from each other by 60°, 90°, 120° or 180° are in sextile, square, trine or opposition aspect, respectively; other signs are not in aspect.[1] The same goes for terms or individual degrees within the signs: the 11th degree of Aries is in sextile to the 11th degrees of Gemini and Aquarius, in square to the 11th degrees of Cancer and Capricorn, and so on.[2]

These relationships are normally measured along the circle of the ecliptic, from the longitude of a planet, without any consideration of latitude. Every planet thus has seven points of aspect distributed over the ecliptic, and as the position of the ecliptic can be located in the sky, so can the aspected points. As discussed in previous chapters, every point on the ecliptic has its own diurnal circle and its own semi-arcs. Once the aspect points have been identified, they may therefore be treated in the same way as the zodiacal position of a planet: they can be brought to the horizon or meridian, or to the proportional place of another planet. This is the direction of an aspect in the zodiac without latitude.

Example: Jupiter, honour and glory

The following chart will illustrate the principle. Jupiter, ruler of the ascendant, is conjunct the Sun (natural significator of fame) in the 9th house, combust but in sect. This placement speaks of a life characterized by religion, philosophy and learning – with particular emphasis on the written and spoken word, as the planets are in Virgo ruled by Mercury.

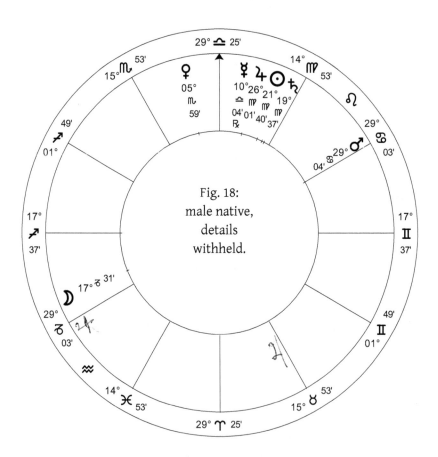

Fig. 18: male native, details withheld.

As Jupiter has a longitude of 26°01', its points of aspect fall in the same degree and minute of their respective signs. Its dexter (right-hand) trine falls in 26°01' Taurus, below the horizon in the 5th house. Its sinister (left-hand) trine falls in 26°01' Capricorn, also below the horizon, but about to rise.

Looking for the exact time when 26°01' Capricorn would be on the ascendant, we find that it was nearly 1 hour and 38 minutes after the time of birth – in other words, 98 minutes. At the rate of 4 minutes for every 1° of right ascension, this yields an arc of direction of 98/4 = 24.5°. We therefore say that the sinister trine of Jupiter is directed to the ascendant around the age of 24y 6m. (Or we may say, in imitation of older authors, that the ascendant is directed to the sinister trine of Jupiter. Only the phrasing differs; the underlying astronomical reality remains the same – cf. Chapter 1.) At this time we would expect the natal significations of Jupiter to manifest in a fortunate manner. Lilly, writing of the direction in general terms, states:

> [I]t produces an augmentation of Fortune, Patrimony, Friendship, Honour and Glory in all the actions of that yeer [...] the Native is in favour with Princes or Nobles, Knights or Gentlemen, according to the capacity of his Birth [...][3]

At the age of 24y 6m, the native published a book – the fruit of more than a decade's study – which won great acclaim and made him a public figure. Within half a year, the book had been shortlisted for the most prestigious literary prize in his country; shortly thereafter, the native was offered and accepted a seat in the national research council.

Aspects as fixed or moving points

In the above example, the place of Jupiter's aspect was the moving element of the direction, while the ascendant was the fixed element. Traditionally, aspects (as well as most planets) have been used only as promissors, and therefore as the moving points in direct directions. Converse directions in the traditional sense, where the significator is moved towards the fixed place of an aspect or other promissor, have been used more sparingly. In my own practice, I have found both kinds of directions to be effective.

Let us continue with the chart in figure 18 and examine the 10th house of profession. This is ruled and occupied by benefic Venus – an indication of professional success. But Venus itself is ruled by a debilitated Mars, which casts a partile and sinister (in both senses of the word) square to the MC itself. While Venus is predisposed to help 10th house matters, Mars is predisposed to harm them.

Immediately after birth, the sinister square of Mars began its descent from the midheaven; and after some 99 minutes, it had reached the natal position of Jupiter, ruler of the ascendant. This corresponds to an arc of 99/4 = 24.75° of right ascension. Shortly before his 25th birthday, the native had applied for a position at a leading university. At the age of 25y 1m, his application was disqualified, and he was taken out of the running for the position on grounds which were later proven to be false. Here the promissor – the square of Mars, threatening harm to professional prospects – is the moving element, while Jupiter, the significator of the native, remains fixed. The direction is in direct motion.

At the same time, Jupiter itself had moved away from its natal position. Some 101 minutes after birth it reached the position which in the natal chart was occupied by 5°59′ Leo. This is the dexter square of Venus, ruler of the 10th in the 10th. Here the significator Jupiter is the moving element, while the promissor – the square of Venus – remains fixed. The direction is therefore said to be in converse motion. The 101 minutes correspond to 101/4 = 25.25° of right ascension. On the basis of this direction, the native, who had put in a new application for an equivalent position, was told that he would get it after initial obstacles; and so he did, at the age of 25y 8m. The positive outcome was due to the contact of two natural benefics ruling the 1st and 10th houses; the initial difficulties, to the nature of the square aspect.

Zodiacal aspects with latitude

As mentioned in Chapter 2, ancient and medieval astrologers were aware that planets differ in their latitudes, and considered these differences to have an effect on the planets' mutual aspects both natally and in directions. 'Umar aṭ-Ṭabarī (8th – 9th century) wrote:

> Dorotheus thought that when the Hyleg is joined to a malefic by the square or opposition aspect, and the malefic is remote in latitude from the path of [the] Hyleg [...] it will not corrupt the lord of the nativity, but will cause it danger. And you should not make a direction without the knowledge of the latitude of the planet [...][4]

A few centuries later, ar-Rijāl objected to the view that directions between planets with different latitudes must be less effective:

> I say that Dorotheus and Abū Maʿshar and al-Hamdānī, and all others who followed their opinions, say that a distance (*remotio*) in the opposition between two planets when the latitude of one of them is northerly, and the latitude of the other southerly, is no joining (*applicatio*) [between them], on account of the difference in the degrees of latitude. Which I reject and say that they were mistaken, using this argument: If any planet should

be in the second degree of Aries, and its latitude northerly, and another planet should be in the second degree of Libra, and its latitude southerly, there will be a true joining from the opposition, just as we have proved in our tables, which we have arranged in this way and made according to our considerations.[5]

Despite the awareness of latitude and the importance ascribed to it in interpretation, the aspect places as such were normally reckoned along the ecliptic without any latitude. With the rise of mundane directions in the 15th century, however, some astrologers felt that aspects as well as conjunctions should be given latitude, so that the place of an aspect could be calculated as a point in space near, but not necessarily on, the ecliptic.

Several methods were proposed for ascribing latitude to aspects. Perhaps the most straightforward method is that ascribed to Bianchini (fl. 1430, also known by the Latinized form Blanchinus). A great circle, known as an aspect circle, is drawn through each planet that has latitude. This circle is inclined to the ecliptic by the latitude of the planet; in other words, the planet is situated at the circle's point of maximum deviation from the ecliptic. The opposition aspect is located 180° away along the aspect circle, at the end of a straight line drawn from the planet through the earth. The opposition will therefore have the same degree and minute of latitude as the planet itself, but of the opposite kind: northern if the planet is southern, and vice versa. All other points of aspect are similarly located along the aspect circle. The squares, 90° distant from the planet, will always coincide with the points where the aspect circle intersects the ecliptic; hence, their latitude will be 0°. The trines and sextiles will have half the latitude of the planet itself – the sextiles being located on the same side (north or south) of the ecliptic as the planet, the trines on the opposite side.

In figure 18 above, Venus in Scorpio has a latitude of -2°14' (negative here meaning south of the ecliptic). Its opposition in Taurus will therefore have a latitude of +2°14' (north of the ecliptic), while the squares in Leo and Aquarius by definition are on the ecliptic with 0° latitude. The two sextiles in Virgo and Capricorn have a latitude of -1°07'; the two trines in Cancer and Pisces, +1°07'. The directions of these aspect points are calculated just like directions of planets with latitude.

Morin agreed with Bianchini's method in locating the aspects of any planet along a circle inclined to the ecliptic, but defined that circle in a more complex manner. The inclination of the aspect circle, according to Morin, should not be the *natal* latitude of the planet casting the aspects, but rather the *preceding or subsequent* maximum latitude of that planet (depending on whether it was decreasing or increasing in latitude at the time of birth). Morin put great faith in this method of 'correcting' aspects for latitude; but, as noted by Holden, the margin of error even in the best ephemerides available in Morin's time makes the value of his experiences with it doubtful.[6]

As mentioned in the preceding chapter, zodiacal aspects with latitude are different from the so-called *mundane aspects* of Placidus, which will be discussed in Chapter 8. Placidus took little interest in the correction of zodiacal aspects for latitude, stating that:

> [...] from the great difference of latitude of such stars as are mutually aspected, there follows some difference of the ray's longitude, but of a very few minutes, which may be omitted; however, those who wish for further investigation, may consult Regiomontanus and Maginus.[7]

Major and minor directions

In Chapter 4 we looked at directions of the planets to the angles, to each other's places, and to intermediate house cusps; and in this chapter we have examined the directions of the aspects. Even without the several innovations introduced in the 17th century (see Chapter 8), these varieties make up a substantial number of directions in any chart – greater than the number of major events in most people's lives. How do we distinguish between important and not-so-important directions?

One method is that of Ptolemy, reducing the number of significators to a bare minimum: the ascendant, midheaven, Sun, Moon, and Part of Fortune. This method was followed by many or most medieval authors, but on the basis of my own experience I must side with ar-Rijāl, Morin and others against it. Rather, I would stress once more the importance of thoroughly analysing the natal chart before attempting to interpret the directions. The radical configuration of the chart will indicate not only the nature of each planet's probable effects, but also its magnitude or importance in life, and therefore in directions.

Planets which are prominent in the radix, for instance by ruling important houses (primarily the ascendant) or by angularity, tend to give pronounced effects. The same is true of directions involving reinforcement: good aspects from dignified benefics, or evil aspects from debilitated malefics. It is also important to note radical aspects, as these will manifest at the time of a direction. Two planets directed to a sextile aspect will give worse results than expected if connected by a natal square; conversely, planets directed to a square will give better results than expected when natally in trine.

SUMMARY

❖ Traditionally, aspects are relations between (similar degrees in) zodiacal signs, and therefore measured along the ecliptic. As points on the ecliptic, aspect places are directed in the same way as the zodiacal position of a planet.

❖ Aspects have been used only as promissors, and therefore as the moving points in direct directions. In converse directions, which were used more sparingly, aspects and other promissors are the fixed points.

❖ To ancient and medieval astrologers, the latitude of a planet affected the interpretation, but not the timing, of a direction. During the Renaissance, some astrologers began ascribing latitude to aspect points according to different principles. This will alter the time of a direction somewhat, but generally not enough for the merit or demerit of the method to be obvious.

❖ The most important directions in a chart are those involving the planets most prominent in the radix, such as the ruler of the ascendant, angular planets, and planets strongly indicating good or evil results by their nature, dignities, rulerships, placement and aspects.

REFERENCES

1. The nature of each aspect is determined by the ruler of the signs in the same relationship to the signs ruled by the luminaries. Beginning from Cancer and Leo, respectively, Taurus and Libra are in sextile aspect; therefore, the sextile has the nature of Venus, the lesser benefic. Similarly, the square has the nature of Mars, the lesser malefic, ruling Aries and Scorpio; the trine has the nature of Jupiter, the greater benefic, ruling Pisces and Sagittarius; and the opposition has the nature of Saturn, the greater malefic, ruling Capricorn and Aquarius.

2. Aspects from degree to degree were used even in Hellenistic astrology, although orbs as we know them today were not.

3. Lilly 1659:658.

4. Hand 1997:16. The hyleg or significator of life will be discussed in Chapter 9.

5. Abenragel 1551:160. *Elhemedeni* mentioned in the Latin text probably refers to the South Arabian geographer, historian and astronomer Abū Muḥammad al-Ḥasan ibn Aḥmad ibn Yaʿqūb al-Hamdānī, c. 893 – 945. I have not seen the tables to which ar-Rijāl refers. It is possible, but not certain, that they contain an early instance of the correction of aspects for latitude discussed below.

6. Holden 1994:188.

7. Cooper [1814] 2004:50.

6

The Quest for Precision

In our example charts so far, we have equated every 4 minutes of clock time following birth with 1° in the rotation of the earth (1° of right ascension passing over the meridian), and every 1° with 1 year of life events. It is now time to become a little more precise.

The time required for the earth to complete a rotation around its axis is not actually 24 hours, but 23h 56m of clock time, known as a sidereal day. (The extra 4 minutes of our civil day are to compensate for the daily secondary motion of the Sun – approximately 1° – in the opposite direction.) Properly speaking, therefore, 1° of right ascension corresponds not to 4 minutes of time, but to 23h 56m / 360° = 3m 59.333s. More importantly, many astrologers consider the original formula of 1° = 1 year to be a mere approximation, and various methods of defining the relationship between degrees of right ascension and years of life more exactly have been suggested. Such definitions are often referred to as *keys*.

The key of Ptolemy

The equation of 1° of right ascension with exactly 1 solar year is generally known as the key of Ptolemy, although it is not of his invention. This was the common measure used in antiquity and for most of the Middle Ages. Older authors often state that by this measure, every month corresponds to 5 minutes of arc (since 1° = 60′, and 60′/12 = 5′) and every day to 10 seconds of arc (since 1′ = 60″, therefore 5′ = 300″, and 300″/30 = 10″). This is not entirely correct, as a true year is not made up of 12 months of 30 days each, but it is close enough and facilitates mental arithmetic.

Let us return to our calculation example from Chapter 4 (fig. 16). For the direction of Mars to the conjunction of Mercury in the zodiac, the arc of direction was 5.83°, or 5°50′. Using the key of Ptolemy, we see that this corresponds to an age of 5y 10m, or – using the rather more correct (though still approximate) value of 365.25 days per year – 5y 304d. The major event related to this direction was an attack of acute appendicitis which occurred about half a year later, at 6y 127d.

The key of Naibod

The second most common key is named after Valentin Naibod (1527 – 1593), but was probably used before his time. It is based on the cycles of the Sun defining both a day (by its primary motion) and a year (by its secondary motion). The Sun completes a full circle of right ascension (360°) in a year, so that the mean distance covered in the course of a day is 360°/365.25, or approximately 0°59′08″. This measure, just under 1°, is taken to represent 1 year of life in primary directions, thereby achieving a fractal-like correspondence of the part to the whole. Most other keys are variations on this principle.[1]

Using Naibod's key, our directional arc of 5°50′ would then correspond to 5°50′/0°59′08″, which is approximately 5.919 years of age, or 5 years 336 days – a difference of only 32 days from the key of Ptolemy. However, the deviation is cumulative, increasing by some 5.25 days for every year of life, so that around the native's age of 70, there will be a whole year's discrepancy between the two keys. For this reason, events in later life are better suited for determining the merits of the respective keys than early events.

The key of Brahe

Naibod's key was further adjusted by Tyge or Tycho Brahe (1546 – 1601), who equated a year of life not with the *mean* distance travelled by the Sun in a day, but with the *actual* distance it covered during the day of birth.[2] This daily motion, measured in right ascension, varies slightly with the time of year. For this purpose, a day is defined as the time between two successive anti-culminations of the Sun (true midnight).

In our example, the right ascension of the Sun at the true midnight preceding birth was 147°56′57″, and at the following midnight, 148°52′39″. The difference between these two values is 0°55′42″. This is the true motion of the Sun in right ascension for the birthday. Dividing the arc of direction (5°50′) by this value, the result is 6.284 years of age, or 6y 104d.

Morin reports having devised and experimented with the same method independently of Brahe, but rejected it on empirical grounds in favour of the key of Naibod.[3] In this he was joined by William Lilly, who, after explaining the keys of Ptolemy and Brahe (as presented by Maginus), concludes:

> The third and the last Measure of time which I now intend to handle, was perfected by *Valentine Naibods* in his Comment of *Ptolomey*, but commended and published by *Maginus* himself, as the more correct and certain measure [...] and in my own judgement it is the most exactest measure that hitherto hath been found out.[4]

My own experience seems tentatively to corroborate this opinion; see the chart of Pope Benedict XVI discussed at the end of this chapter.

The key of Placidus

An even more complex key than that of Brahe was proposed by Placidus, who wanted the distance (in right ascension) travelled by the Sun during the first day after birth to correspond to the first year of life; its distance on the second day, to the second year; etc.[5] To find out the time at which a primary direction is perfected, we must examine how long after birth the Sun would cover an arc of right ascension corresponding to the arc of direction. This number of days (with fractions) is then converted into years.

In our example, the right ascension of the Sun at birth was 147°58'30", to which we add the arc of direction, 5°50'. The resulting degree is 153°48'30", which was reached by the Sun 6d 7h 39m after birth – about 6.319 days. The direction would therefore perfect at the age of 6.319 years, or 6y 117d. This is the closest match yet. Unfortunately, however, such close hits are not very common with any key – which leads us to our next consideration.

Limitations in timing

In previous chapters, we have been content to note simply in what year of a native's life a primary direction is completed. In doing so, we have in fact taken a traditional stance: astrologers of earlier times never attempted to use directions alone for more precise timing. Nevertheless, contemporary astrologers interested in primary directions sometimes claim consistently to achieve hit dates corresponding to the actual week or day of an event. Such claims may sound impressive, but typically do not hold up under investigation.[6] The observation made by Morin more than 350 years ago still holds true:

And experience proves that [...] the accident (i.e., event) sometimes comes before the precise time of the direction, and sometimes follows it; not by one day only, or one month, but even by several, or rather now and then throughout the year, although this happens more rarely; and this [happens with] whatever may be taken as the measure of that arc and howsoever the aspects of the planets are corrected (for latitude). For there is no nativity in which the effects of all the directions correspond exactly in time to their arcs; and very frequently it happens that if in any nativity two or three such directions are seen, the rest will in fact be found to precede or follow [the time of their effects] more or less.[7]

By increasing the varieties of directional methods and keys used, as well as the number of planets, aspects, and other points included – a development which began during Morin's lifetime – we can produce such a wealth of directions that almost any event will fall within a few days of some direction or other; but this does not necessarily make for better astrology. A direction is connected astrologically to an event not simply by proximity in time, but by the natures of the planets involved and their significations in the natal chart. As discussed in Chapter 1, the understanding of each planet's natal promise forms the basis of all prediction.

In Morin's view there were several reasons for discrepancies in the timing of directions, the imperfect nature of the astronomical tables available in the 17th century being only one of these. According to Morin, planets which are slow by nature (such as Saturn) or weakened in the natal chart tend to give their results after the expected time, while those which are swift by nature (such as the Moon) or strong in the chart give their results early. Most importantly, however, the timing of a direction may be affected by other predictive methods – operating closer, as it were, to the human sphere. Directions must therefore be combined with such other techniques. This, indeed, is the consensus among older astrological authors. In Chapter 10, we shall examine some of the methods used to pinpoint the time of an event indicated by primary directions.

Directions as single events or periods

Perhaps the most important reason for directions not tallying exactly with the time of this or that event is that a single event does not typically exhaust the meaning of the direction. Rather, a primary direction indicates a planetary influence operating over an extended period of time. During this period the native may experience several events corresponding to the meanings of the significator and promissor, although outwardly unrelated.

One example of this phenomenon was given in Chapter 4, figure 15, where Mars in the 1st house as ruler of the 10th directed to the ascendant signified both a severe fever and employment. These were both major events, remembered many years later. A closer look at such a period might also reveal a series of minor events which may not be so well remembered, but which bear the obvious imprint of the planet or planets involved – in the case of a Mars direction to the ascendant, minor injuries or burns, irritability, disputes, and so forth.

The view of primary directions as indicating periods is most apparent in the technique of directing the ascendant through the terms (or bounds) of the signs – or, more astronomically phrased, directing the terms of the signs to the eastern horizon. As discussed in Chapter 2, this technique is found in the oldest sources on directions, and was still in use in the 17th century.

Example: Joseph Ratzinger's rise to the papacy
As was said above, the difference between most 'keys' will increase over time, so that it is most noticeable for events in old age.[8] Let us look, then, at a very major event in the life of an old man: Joseph Ratzinger, now Pope Benedict XVI.

Even to a beginning student of astrology, this chart (fig. 19) carries the signature of a religious dignitary. Jupiter, natural significator of religion, rules the 10th house of dignities and is powerfully situated on the ascendant, while Saturn – ruler of the ascendant and of Jupiter – is in the 9th house of religion. The Jupiter-Saturn emphasis is particularly fitting for a man known for his religious austerity and nicknamed 'der Panzer-Kardinal'. Of almost equal importance, however, is the partile trine aspect from the exalted Sun – natural significator of glory and honours – to the MC, promising public recognition.

As Ratzinger rose to the highest position of honour and power possible within the Catholic Church and became one of the most public figures in the world just after his 78th birthday, we should expect to see primary directions involving these same planets around that time. In particular, we should look to Jupiter, which rules the MC and has a natural affinity with dignity (especially ecclesiastical dignity), and to the Sun, which closely

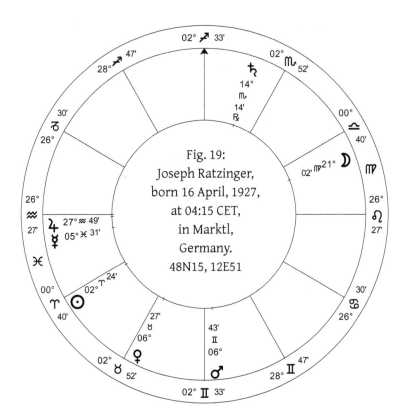

Fig. 19:
Joseph Ratzinger,
born 16 April, 1927,
at 04:15 CET,
in Marktl,
Germany.
48N15, 12E51

aspects the MC and has a natural affinity with power and fame, enhanced by exaltation.

As a matter of fact, the trine of Jupiter (without latitude) was directed to the Sun with an arc of 76.72°, or 76°43′, using proportional semi-arcs. (The corresponding arc using Regiomontanian circles of position is 74°08′.) Converting this arc to dates according to the four keys discussed above, we see that they give the following results:

Ptolemy	5 January, 2004
Naibod	16 February, 2005
Brahe	17 May, 2010
Placidus	27 March, 2004

Ratzinger was elected Pope on 19 April, 2005, a time which agrees most closely with the Naibod key. We shall return to this chart in Chapter 10.

SUMMARY

❖ 1° of primary motion (the rotation of the earth around its axis) is completed in 3m 59.333s of clock time.

❖ The earliest practice in symbolically converting degrees to time, prevalent up to the Renaissance and still widespread, was to equate 1 year of life with exactly 1° of primary motion. This is the 'key of Ptolemy'.

❖ The second most common option is the 'key of Naibod', equating 1 year of life with 0°59'08", the mean motion of the Sun in right ascension during 1 day. This was the measure preferred by Jean-Baptiste Morin and William Lilly.

❖ The 'key of Brahe' equates 1 year of life with the true motion of the Sun in right ascension for the birthday, which varies slightly with the time of year.

❖ The 'key of Placidus' equates each year of life with the true motion of the Sun in right ascension for the corresponding day after birth.

❖ The difference between the first three 'keys' will increase over time, so that it is most noticeable for events in old age. The key of Placidus is less predictable.

❖ Traditional astrological authors used primary directions only to determine the probable year of an event, using other astrological techniques to define the time more closely. Modern claims of extreme accuracy for primary directions alone tend not to hold up under investigation.

❖ Primary directions do not necessarily indicate discrete events, but rather influences operating over a period of time. During such a period, several seemingly unrelated events corresponding to the meanings of the significator and promissor may be experienced. This perspective harmonizes with the earliest use of primary directions.

REFERENCES

1. According to Morin (Holden 1994:81), Cardan was of the same opinion as Naibod. Kolev s.a:35, however, gives the key of Cardan as 0°59′12″ per year, based on the division of 360° by 365 whole days (which more correctly yields 0°59′11″). Neither gives any explicit reference to Cardan's works.

2. Brahe's key is sometimes called the key of Johannes Kepler (1571 – 1630, a pupil of Brahe), but was in fact described by Brahe himself in his *De Stella Nova* (1573). Morin quotes Kepler as advocating, on theoretical grounds, a 'key' which in fact amounts to an entirely new technique of direction, known today as 'solar arc directions' and only partly based on the primary motion – an idea rejected by Morin in no uncertain terms (Holden 1994:79 f). For more information on Kepler's methods, see Strauß & Strauß-Kloebe [1926] 1981.

3. Holden 1994:78 ff.

4. Lilly 1659:712.

5. Placidus' key is obviously linked to his 'secondary directions'; cf. Chapter 2. It may be objected that all the primary directions corresponding to a human life-span are completed within hours of birth, and are therefore unrelated to the motion of the Sun on subsequent days.

6. A case in point is a recent anonymous volume on rectification techniques, which states that we must 'discard any notion [that] the *orb* surrounding a primary direction to the angles may last several months or a year [...] directions to the angles for a reliably timed birth chart occur within a few days, often within 48 hours' (Regulus 2008:299). By this means among others, the author claims to have rectified the birth times of American presidents to the very second. Unfortunately, the calculations on which this claim is based were incorrectly performed, so that many of the supposed directions are invalid, and others have a large error margin. By way of illustration, the very first chart in the database (that of George Washington, Regulus 2008:422 ff) contains seven supposed primary directions to the angles. Five of these are incorrectly calculated, bringing the ecliptical degrees of the natal angles to the promissors rather than the promissors to the fixed angles, and assigning aspects to the angles rather than to the planets. Of the remaining two directions, Jupiter's zodiacal opposition to the ascendant is wrong by 1 year 9 months, perfecting around 17 January, 1771, rather

than the stated time of 21 April, 1769. Only the very last direction, the zodiacal sextile of Mars to the midheaven, is correct within a few days.

7. Holden 1994:89. Insertions in round brackets are mine.

8. The key of Placidus is variable, so that its period of maximum variation from any other key may occur at any time in life.

Getting Technical: More Variables

The preceding chapters cover the fundamentals of primary directions as they were practised from classical antiquity up to the Renaissance. This practice was presumably based partly on theoretical considerations, partly on a wish for mathematical simplicity and feasibility. In the current age of computers, the latter factor need no longer concern us. We are therefore free to determine the best method of directions on the basis of theoretical principles and empirical results. The problems discussed in this chapter all deal with the question of whether observable planetary positions should be preferred over idealized or standardized ones, or vice versa.

Secondary motion

In our example charts so far, all directed planets have been regarded as fixed in their natal zodiacal positions. In the few hours after birth during which all directions are perfected, six of the seven traditional planets move only minutes or even seconds of arc along the ecliptic – an amount which translates into a few weeks or months of life at most. The Moon, however, is different: two hours after birth, corresponding to some 30 years of age, its position may have changed by a degree or more, shifting the time of a projected event by over a year. This clearly makes secondary motion a problem worth considering, at least in directions involving the Moon, despite the fact that is has generally been ignored.

The argument *against* including secondary motion is based on a wholly spatial or non-temporal definition of primary directions. On this view, the actual *motion* of the promissor towards the natal place of the significator in the hours following birth is of no interest. Only the natal *distance* between promissor and significator (whether a great circle or a proportional point), measured in degrees of right ascension along the diurnal circle of the promissor, matters. This perspective is quite untraditional, and particularly at variance with Ptolemy's time-based proportional semi-arc method.[1] It also opens the door for the modern understanding of 'converse' directions (cf. Chapter 8).

Some modern writers on primary directions have made allowances for the secondary motion of the Moon only as promissor, and not as significator. But if the actual motion of the Moon after birth is to be used in calculating arcs of direction, it must, for the sake of consistency, also be used in calculating the Moon's own semi-arc and its proportional position – either as promissor or as significator – within that semi-arc. In other words, the semi-arcs must be based on the actual rising, setting, culmination and anti-culmination times of the Moon (whether *in mundo* or *in zodiaco*).

Lunar parallax

Another problem relevant mostly with regard to the Moon is *parallax*. This is the difference between the apparent positions of a planet as observed from a *topocentric* perspective (somewhere on the earth's surface) or calculated from the *geocentric* perspective (the centre of the earth) – cf. Chapter 3. The extent of the parallax depends on the relative distances between the points of observation and the planet observed. Most planets are so far away from the earth that the difference between their topocentric and geocentric positions at any time is negligible; but in the case of the Moon, the difference can amount to about 1° of longitude when the Moon is near the horizon (gradually decreasing as it approaches the meridian).

Astrology is topocentric by nature: for the purpose of casting a natal chart, the place of birth is regarded as the centre of the cosmos. Nevertheless, throughout history astrologers have typically used the geocentric, universal – and therefore only approximate – position of the Moon for their charts, presumably for reasons of mathematical simplicity. This seems to be true even of astrologers who explicitly advocated correction for parallax, such as Morin and Placidus.[2]

Refraction

For planets near the horizon, parallax is not the only issue to be considered. The phenomenon known as *atmospheric refraction*, caused by variations in air density as light passes through the atmosphere, makes such planets appear higher in the sky than astronomical calculation would indicate. The planets therefore seem to rise earlier and set later. The maximum refraction is just above half a degree, and the consideration of refraction can therefore affect the timing of some primary directions by up to half a year; but like secondary motion and parallax, it has typically been ignored by astrologers. Approximate refraction values – and therefore approximate times of apparent rising and setting – can be calculated by astrological software; but the exact values vary slightly with local temperature and pressure conditions.

Planetary size

A final consideration concerns the size of the planets. Both ancient and modern ephemerides (as well as astrological software) treat all planets as points, using the centre of a planet's disc to trace its motion through the zodiac. In reality, however, the visible discs of the planets vary in extension from a few seconds of arc up to about half a degree for the Sun and Moon. When we direct either of the luminaries to a great circle such as the horizon or meridian, the leading edge of its disc will therefore touch the circle some 0°15′ (half the luminary's diameter) before its centre does, corresponding to a difference of about three months in the timing of its effect. The body of the luminary will then travel across the circle for about six months in all. If the luminaries are directed to each other, the disc of the promissor will overlap with the natal place of the significator's disc for a full year.

In directing by circles of position as discussed in Chapter 4, consideration of disc size for the Sun or Moon as fixed point will cause such a circle to expand into a 'band of position' some 0°30′ wide (0°15′ to either side of the original circle). As a promissor will nearly always cross this band at an oblique angle, the actual duration of such a direction may be considerably longer, amounting to nearly a year – more, if the promissor in question is the other luminary.

Example: the Moon rises again
As the problems just considered most affect the Moon and planets near the horizon, let us return to the very first example chart in Chapter 1, where the Moon is in the 1st house as ruler of the 10th, about to rise over the horizon.

At the age of 29y 0m, the native graduated from university; some 6 months later, he gained an academic appointment. What set of criteria will match the direction of the Moon to the ascendant most closely with this period? To some extent this depends on the chosen time-key, but the table below will show the arcs of direction resulting from the combination of various considerations: latitude, secondary motion, parallax correction, atmospheric refraction, and disc size (using the edge of the Moon rather than its centre).

Latitude	No	No	No	No	Yes	Yes	Yes	Yes
Sec. mot.	No	No	Yes	Yes	No	Yes	No	Yes
Parallax	No	Yes	No	Yes	No	No	Yes	Yes
Refr./size	No	No	No	No	No	No	No	Yes
Arc of direction	22°20′	23°31′	23°47′	24°59′	27°07′	28°11′	29°11′	29°24′

Perhaps not surprisingly, given the fundamentally observational nature of astrology, the time of observable moonrise gives the closest match.[3]

SUMMARY

❖ Some calculations traditionally employed in primary directions, and in astrology generally, deviate from the observable positions and movements of the planets and have apparently come into use as a means of simplification.

❖ For the purposes of primary directions, the secondary motion of most planets except the Moon is negligible. The same is true of parallax, which is the difference between the topocentric and geocentric perspectives in determining a planet's position.

❖ The effect of lunar parallax is most marked near the horizon. This is also true of atmospheric refraction, which makes any planet in this region appear higher in the sky than calculation would indicate.

❖ Viewing the Sun and Moon as discs rather than points will increase the duration of their directions. The disc size of the other planets is too small to be of much importance.

❖ The combination of all these factors can alter the time of some directions by several years.

REFERENCES

1. Nevertheless, it was passionately defended by Erich Carl Kühr, who taught a modified version of that method. Kühr's views are worth quoting and examining in brief:

   Every place occupied at the moment of birth retains its character unchanged for the entire duration of life [...] According to this fundamental proposition, no radical place must be moved, for every movement contravenes the fundamental proposition. It is certainly astonishing that this obvious conclusion has never been drawn before, but that does not alter its correctness. Until now, each direction has been understood – with no realization of one's inconsistency and illogicality – as the movement of one radical place towards another, by which, with advancing age, the radix is increasingly altered [...] The analogous relationship between an aspect and an arc of direction admits the further conclusion that the directions no more require an actual movement to bring them about than do the effects of the radical aspects [...] From this it further follows necessarily that *only radical places* must be directed by primary motion, and never places progressed in the zodiac, as has lately been done by consideration of the motion of the ☽ in the first hours after birth. (Kühr 1936:56, 61)

In Kühr's perception, then, any consideration of the actual planetary movements after the moment for which a chart is fixed would contravene the very idea of a fixed chart. However obvious this reasoning may have seemed to Kühr, it is far from compelling. Astrological tradition does view the chart as a fixed moment in time, but within an ongoing process of celestial motion: the planetary aspects, with which it pleases Kühr to compare arcs of direction, do indeed 'require an actual movement' to bring about their effects, whether of perfection or frustration. Nor is Kühr consistent in his rejection of such process thinking, as he rejects Bianchini's static model of assigning latitude to aspects (cf. Chapter 5) in favour of Morin's, which is based precisely on planetary movements before and after the time of birth (see Kühr 1936:303 ff).

2. Holden 2008a:22 f, 2008b:102 f, and Placidus de Titis 1675:17: ' [...] it follows that the places of the planets are to be examined as taken according to parallax, and not according to the common way, at the centre of the earth, as professors generally opine.'

3. The same is true of the second chart with a rising Moon discussed in Chapter 1.

8

Modern Innovations

In this chapter, we shall examine certain developments in the theory and practice of primary directions from the 17th to the 20th century. We have already met with the consideration of planetary latitude or *in mundo* positions, in general use from the 15th century (discussed in Chapter 4), and with the problems of secondary motion, parallax correction, disk size and refraction (discussed in the previous chapter). While these considerations may be called innovations in so far as they did not form part of the classical and medieval traditions, they all focus on a more exact *observation* of the seven traditional planets. By contrast, the techniques discussed below are the outcome of new mathematical or technological sophistication, and add new elements to primary directions rather than refining existing ones.

New aspects and new planets

In addition to conjunctions, ancient and medieval astrologers worked with the so-called Ptolemaic aspects of sextile (60°), square or quartile (90°), trine or trigon (120°), and opposition (180°), directing the aspect places of each planet as discussed in Chapter 5. In the 17th century, however, astrologers began to invent new aspect angles.

Among the more conservative innovators was Morin, who added only the semi-sextile (30°) and quincunx (150°) to make twelve points of contact in all, each a multiple of 30°.[1] Placidus, taking his cue from 'the very excellent Kepler' in arguing for a connection between astrology and musical harmonies, accepted only the quintile (72°), biquintile (144°) and sesquisquare or sesquiquartile (135°), along with the classical aspects, as powerful – making eight angles (including the conjunction) to match scale intervals.[2] Yet others, such as Lilly, included all of the above and more: the semi-square (45°), semi-quintile (36°, now often called decile), and sesquiquintile (108°, now often called tridecile).[3] Needless to say, such a plethora of aspects will increase the number of directions considerably.

After the discoveries of Uranus (initially known as the Georgian planet or Herschel) in 1781, Neptune in 1846, and Pluto in 1930, some astrologers working with primary directions gradually began to include these bodies among the promissors (and sometimes among the significators), again causing the number of directions during a lifetime to swell significantly.

Mundane 'aspects'

All aspects discussed above are calculated in the zodiac, that is to say, with reference to the ecliptic. Although astrologers of the classical era did recognize certain non-zodiacal relationships, notably that of 'co-rising' stars, *paranatellonta* (παρανατέλλοντα) or *synatellonta* (συνατέλλοντα), these terms were generally applied to the fixed stars rising with particular degrees of the zodiac at a given latitude, rather than to co-rising planets.

Antiochus of Athens (2nd century CE?) describes 'temporal' or 'ascensional' configurations between two planets based on the rising times of the signs – in other words, on oblique ascensions.[4] As the entire zodiac rises in just under 24 hours, planets rising some 8 hours of clock-time apart would form a temporal trine, 8 being one third of 24. Put differently, the oblique ascensions of these planets (the points on the equator rising simultaneously with them) would be 120° apart. Similarly, planets rising 6 hours apart would form a temporal square (90° of oblique ascension); planets rising 4 hours apart, a temporal sextile (60° of oblique ascension); and so on.

'Aspects' such as these do not appear to have been used in directions by ancient or medieval astrologers, although in one much-debated sentence, Ptolemy seems to entertain a notion of ascensional distance *modifying* the nature of zodiacal aspects:

> And sometimes, also, among the signs that ascend slowly the sextile aspect [destroys, when it is] afflicted, and again among the signs that ascend rapidly the trine.[5]

In signs which are slow to rise (often called 'of long ascension'), the rising of 60° of zodiacal longitude over the horizon may approach a temporal square, depending on the latitude of observation; conversely, in signs rising quickly ('of short ascension'), the rising of 120° of zodiacal longitude may do the same. For this reason, Ptolemy apparently sees such aspects as taking on something of the destructive quality of the square aspect.

In the 16th and 17th centuries, however, novel kinds of 'aspects' were proposed, bearing no relation to zodiacal positions. Giovanni Antonio Magini (1555 – 1617), in certain respects a precursor of Placidus, had suggested that aspectual angles might be measured by degrees of right ascension on the equator as well as in the ecliptic. But this model was rejected by Placidus – who regarded it as purely geometrical, and therefore fictional – in favour of what since his time has been called aspects *in mundo* ('in the world'), or simply *mundane aspects*.

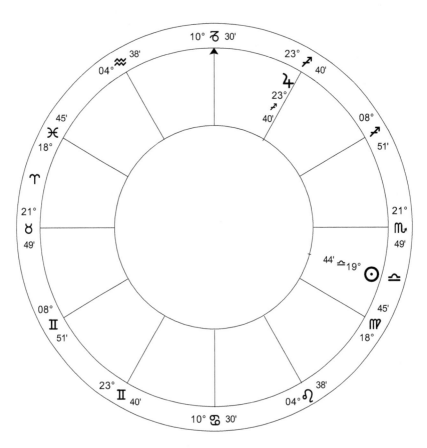

Fig. 20: mundane aspect. Jupiter, having completed one third of its diurnal semi-arc, is conjunct the 9th Placidean cusp. When the Sun by primary direction conjuncts the 6th cusp, it will have completed one third of its nocturnal semi-arc, thereby forming a mundane square to Jupiter's natal position.

Placidus' mundane aspects, like his house system, are based on the Ptolemaic method of direction by proportional semi-arcs.[6] As the 360° diurnal circle of any planet is divided by its cardinal points of rising, culmination, setting, and anti-culmination into four quadrants or semi-arcs (two diurnal or above the horizon, two nocturnal or below it), Placidus equates each such semi-arc with 90°. Any point on the horizon will therefore always be considered to form a mundane square with any point on the meridian; likewise, a planet removed from the horizon by a certain proportion of its semi-arc will form a mundane square with a planet removed from the meridian by an identical proportion of its own semi-arc.

Next, a semi-arc can be divided into three equal parts, each of which is equated with 30°, and which by addition to or subtraction from the mundane square form the mundane trines and sextiles. These thirds of a semi-arc also function as the Placidean houses, so that two planets distant by precisely two Placidus houses (for example, on the cusps of the 9th and 11th, respectively, or both exactly halfway through these houses) are considered to form a mundane sextile. Further division of the planetary semi-arcs serves to define other mundane aspects such as the 72° quintile ($^4/_5$ of a semi-arc), the 135° sesquiquadrate (1½ semi-arc), and so forth.

Placidus thus ends up with a double set of aspects for every planet, one in the zodiac (or 'in the *primum mobile*') and one 'in the world', each set consisting of one opposition and pairs of sextiles, quintiles, squares, trines, sesquisquares and biquintiles. He does not accept any zodiacal aspects to the angles, but allows planets to be directed to each other either by mundane as well as zodiacal aspects (although following Ptolemy in generally regarding only the Sun and Moon among the planets as significators).[7] This too increases the number of directions considerably.

Antiscia and parallels

Like aspects, *antiscia* – sometimes loosely grouped with the aspects – date back to the classical era. These are points on the ecliptic equidistant from the solstitial points (in the tropical zodiac, 0° Cancer and 0° Capricorn), and therefore rising in the same amount of time – in other words, sharing the same diurnal, and nocturnal, arc. The ecliptical point opposite an antiscium is known as a *contrantiscium*. It has a diurnal arc corresponding to the nocturnal arc of the antiscium, and vice versa.

In the 17th century, both Morin and Placidus separately argued that the antiscium of a planet should be calculated not from its zodiacal longitude, but from its actual body: its position *in mundo*.[8] All points sharing the same rising time, whether they are on the ecliptic (as zodiacal degrees are) or not, have the same distance north or south of the equator: they share the same *declination*. Placidus therefore renamed antiscia 'parallels of declination', also known as parallels in the *primum mobile* or in the zodiac. A planet not located exactly on the ecliptic will have two such antiscia or points of parallel declination in the ecliptic: one close to its own degree of zodiacal longitude, and one on the opposite side of the solstice axis.

Two planets or points equally far from the equator but on opposite sides – one north, the other south – form contra-parallels of declination (contrantiscia), as the diurnal arc of one equals the nocturnal arc of the other. Placidus in particular gave much weight to the direction of planetary parallels and contra-parallels in the zodiac to the significators.

To these, Placidus also added two new kinds of parallel based on planetary relations to the angles. In a *mundane parallel* by direct motion, we ask ourselves by how much of its semi-arc a significator is removed from the horizon or meridian. When the promissor reaches a point where the same proportion of its own semi-arc remains on the opposite side of that angle, it has reached the mundane parallel of the significator. If, for instance, the Sun is in the 9th house at birth, having passed exactly $1/10$ of its semi-arc from midheaven to descendant, its mundane parallel will fall on the other side of the meridian; and Venus will have reached it when $1/10$ remains of its own semi-arc from ascendant to midheaven (see fig. 21).

A *rapt parallel* works on the same principle, but takes the primary motion of both planets into consideration. Thus, if the Sun is found in the 2nd house at birth, and Venus in the 3rd, we observe the movement of both until they are located on opposite sides of the ascendant, distant from it by the same proportional amount of their respective semi-arcs. The time elapsed from birth until this happens gives the arc of direction.

Rapt parallels are as time-sensitive as common directions to the angles: on average, they will change by 1 year of life for every 4 minutes of birth time – although in practice these numbers will vary considerably for parallels around the horizon. Other mundane parallels are twice as sensitive to changes, as the position of the promissor will increase, while that of the proportional point to which it is directed will decrease, with every increment in birth time.

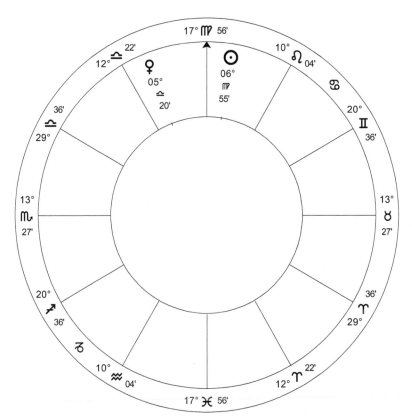

Fig. 21: mundane and rapt parallels. If the Sun is regarded as fixed, Venus
reaching a point at the same proportional distance from the midheaven, but on
the opposite side, constitutes a mundane parallel. If the motion of both planets
is considered, bringing them to the points where they share the same
proportional distance from the midheaven constitutes a rapt parallel.

Placidean poles

Placidus used and advocated the classical Ptolemaic method of directing
planets to each other by proportional semi-arcs, as explained in Chapter
4. Since the calculations involved are cumbersome and time-consuming
to perform by hand, he also published tables which could be used to
approximate semi-arc directions by means of poles and circles of position
– concepts familiar to astrologers of his day, as they were used in the
'rational system' of Regiomontanus. This method, known as *directions
under the pole of the significator*, generally gives dates within a few months of
the Ptolemaic method (but may differ from the Regiomontanian by several

years). By frequently repeated misrepresentations, directions under the pole came to be accepted by many as the 'true' system of Placidus, and came into increasing popularity over the following centuries. Partridge and Worsdale both used them, and among their 19th and 20th century proponents were R. J. Morrison (Zadkiel I), W. R. Old (Sepharial) and E. C. Kühr. Not everyone favoured the method, however. The second Zadkiel, A. J. Pearce, wrote:

> Formerly the Sun and Moon were directed under their poles, and this method is taught in *Zadkiel's Grammar of Astrology*, as well as the method already given of directing those bodies by means of their *semi-arcs*. The latter is the simpler method, and I advise the student always to follow it.[9]

A pole is a point directly above the centre of a circle, at the end of a line perpendicular to the plane of the circle (its axis). The pole of the birth horizon is therefore the zenith of the birth place, and its 'elevation' or declination (distance north or south of the *celestial* equator) equals the geographical latitude of the birth place itself (its distance north or south of the *terrestrial* equator). Similarly, the poles of the meridian circle are the east and west points of the horizon, which always intersect the equator and therefore have 0° declination.

The pole of a planet is measured with reference to its *circle of position*, which is an artificial 'horizon' passing through the body of a planet. Directions under the pole are therefore the same as directions by circles of position. In Chapter 4 we examined the directional method of Regiomontanus, which uses position circles intersecting the north and south points of the natal horizon. The position circles of Placidus are based instead on proportional semi-arcs (just like Placidean houses and Placidean mundane aspects). Each quadrant of the celestial sphere contains one of the planet's four semi-arcs, as well as exactly one fourth of the celestial equator, or 90° of right ascension. A Placidean circle of position is defined as passing through both the body of a planet and a point on the equator proportional to the planet's position in its semi-arc.

Thus, if Jupiter in the 10th house of the chart has traversed ¾ of its diurnal semi-arc or path from the horizon to the meridian, then Jupiter's proportional point on the equator will be ¾ (or 67°30′) removed from the horizon – in other words, 22°30′ from the meridian – in the same quadrant. A great circle passing through this proportional point as well as through Jupiter itself constitutes Jupiter's Placidean circle of position. This circle will necessarily intersect the *diurnal* circles of all other planets. When any planet (or other point, such as a place of aspect) reaches its intersection with Jupiter's circle of position, it is considered to be conjunct Jupiter by primary motion.

Crepuscular and obscure arcs

To Placidus, light was the medium through which the influence of the heavenly bodies is transmitted to us. This belief led him to advocate special procedures in directions to the Sun, whose light is visible for some time before its rising and after its setting.

When the Sun is below the horizon by less than 18° of altitude, it is said to be in the *crepuscular* (twilight) space. In such cases, Placidus wanted the moving element of the direction to be brought not to the corresponding point in its semi-arc, but rather to the same circle of altitude as the Sun. These circles, parallel to the horizon, are known as *crepuscular* (or *crepusculine*) *arcs*. As they are below the horizon their altitude is expressed by a negative number, and is sometimes known as *depression*.

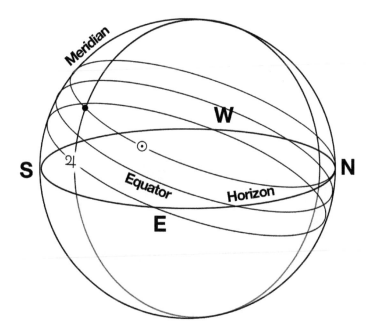

Fig. 22: The diurnal circle of the Sun intersecting Jupiter's Placidean circle of position (which does not coincide with the north and south points of the horizon).

To calculate a direction to the Sun in the crepuscular space, Placidus would first compute the distance in oblique ascension between the moving point (generally a planet or aspect) and the Sun. Next, the horizontal distance of the Sun would be computed, as well as the horizontal distance which the moving point would have when in the Sun's circle of altitude. Finally, the difference between these two, known as the *ortive difference*, would be added to or subtracted from the original distance to obtain the arc of direction.

When the Sun is more than 18° below the horizon, it is said to be in the *obscure space*. In directing a planet or aspect to such a Sun, Placidus would first compute the part of the Sun's nocturnal semi-arc located within the crepuscular space (-18° of altitude) and subtract that from the full semi-arc; the remainder is the Sun's *obscure arc*. He would then do the same for the point directed to the Sun. Thereafter the direction would be calculated by proportional obscure arcs, rather than proportional semi-arcs.

These procedures of Placidus' have not found much favour even among his own adherents. Some have criticized his manner of calculating the special arcs, while others – a majority – have rejected them altogether.[10] They are rarely if ever used today.

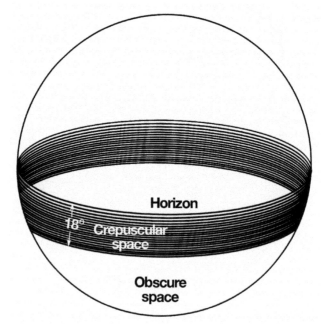

Fig. 23: The crepuscular and obscure arcs according to Placidus.

The Part of Fortune

The mathematically derived points known as Lots, and later as (Arabic) Parts, were much used in both Hellenistic and medieval Perso-Arabic astrology; but the only one mentioned by Ptolemy is the Lot, or Part, of Fortune. This point was used in calculations of longevity, discussed in the next chapter, and has figured prominently in the history of primary directions.

The Part of Fortune was traditionally regarded as a point on the ecliptic and directed as such even by astrologers who favoured directions *in mundo* for planets with latitude. Morin, for instance, stated that 'it is certain and verified by many experiences that its directions are efficacious [...] and the Part of Fortune itself is allotted the function of significator in directions as well as the function of promissor'.[11]

Placidus, however, disagreed. 'I willingly confess', he wrote, 'that, with regard to the ⊕ I have laboured a long time, and have not been able hitherto to find any truth in it'.[12] Convinced by his admiration for Ptolemy that the truth must nevertheless be there to find, Placidus sought to reinterpret Ptolemy's statement that the Part of Fortune should be a 'lunar ascendant', always as far distant from the Moon as the ascendant is from the Sun.[13]

Placidus' first attempt at finding an alternative Part was to project its position not along the ecliptic, which is the Sun's apparent orbit through the zodiac, but along the corresponding orbit of the Moon. He abandoned this model, however, to embrace the one proposed by Adriano Negusanti of Fano, Italy (d. 1685), who wanted the Part to be projected along the Moon's circle of declination.[14] This mode of calculation results in the Part generally occupying a point in space distant not only from the ecliptic, but from the zodiac as a whole, which is why followers of Placidus have sometimes declined to assign any zodiacal position to it.[15]

Being located outside of the zodiac, the Placidean Part of Fortune cannot receive any zodiacal aspects. At the same time, the Part lacks the so-called rapt motion: it is not carried around the world from east to west during the course of a day, and would thus be unable to form any rapt or mundane parallels or mundane aspects.[16] The Part is therefore restricted to the passive role of receiving the mundane aspects of other planets and sharing parallels of declination with them, the declination of the Part being always identical with that of the Moon.[17]

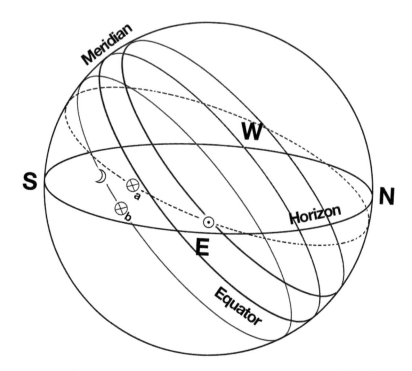

Fig. 24: The Part of Fortune calculated by the traditional method (a) and according to Placidus (b).

Converse directions

As discussed in Chapter 1, a 'converse' direction was traditionally understood as bringing the significator with the primary motion to the place of the promissor rather than vice versa. In both cases, the movement was caused by the daily rotation of the celestial sphere from east to west – or, in modern terms, by the rotation of the earth around its axis. Naturally, the significator in question would have to be a point which could move with this primary motion, such as a planet, and not an immovable circle such as the horizon or meridian.

In the 17th century, however, some astrologers began to direct the *zodiacal degrees* on the natal ascendant or midheaven to the planets and their aspects, calling this the 'converse direction of the angles'. Thus, for a person born with 15° Virgo on the ascendant, the ecliptical point of 15° Virgo would be directed with the primary motion to planets and their aspect points. At the close of the century, Partridge wrote of this method:

> They have a new invented way to direct the Ascendent and Midheaven
> Convers; by which Method they discover their ignorance in Directional
> Motion [...] This Method I have seen used in Nativities by some of our
> Modern Professors; but the first Author I find it in, is *Morinus* [...][18]

Although the method was not standard procedure, Morin was not actually
the first astrologer to have advocated it: ar-Rijāl had done the same some
five hundred years earlier, citing in its support an anonymous nativity
with Leo ascending and the Moon conjunct a nebulous star in Cancer: 'And
when the direction of the Moon arrived at the degree of the ascendant, it
made the native blind in the beginning of his fortieth year.'[19]

Placidus, on the other hand, rejected not only converse directions
of natally angular degrees, but also of zodiacal aspects, on the grounds
that these are perfected by forward motion in the zodiac. In directing
conversely, he therefore employed only his self-invented mundane aspects
(see above).

At some point during the late 19th or early 20th century, the very
meaning of the term 'converse' underwent a drastic transformation. Wilson,
writing in 1819, still defines converse motion as 'when the Significator is
moved from east to west by the diurnal motion of the Earth'.[20] Oxley, in
1830, illustrates the same understanding in his examples, as does Worsdale
in his.[21] But a later generation of writers, criticizing this traditional use of
the term, proposed an entirely different definition:

> According to one system, *direct* directions are those in which a planet [i.e.,
> promissor] is directed to an aspect of the Sun or Moon [i.e., the significator];
> while those in which the Sun or Moon is directed to an aspect of a planet are
> described as *converse*. This nomenclature is quite arbitrary and has proved
> confusing to most students as well as to many writers on the subject [...] we
> call that direct which seems to imply normal motion clockwise through the
> houses under the influence of axial rotation [...] and that is called converse
> which appears (whatever may be the true explanation of it) to require the
> heavenly body to move anti-clockwise in a manner contrary to that which
> is caused by axial rotation [...].[22]

The 'neo-converse' directions, then, consist in mentally reversing the
rotation of the earth, or the course of time, so that a direction perfecting
two hours (30°) *before* birth would correspond to a life event taking place
30 years *after* birth. Leo further seems to have been unaware of the great
difference between this method and the one proposed by Morin and

others. Taking the chart of Theosophist leader Annie Besant (fig. 25) as an example, he wrote:

> The earth rotates from west to east, and when a planet is situated just below the cusp of the ascendant, like Uranus in this horoscope, axial rotation will make it appear to rise through the twelfth, eleventh, and tenth houses, forming direct directions as it does so. In order for it to form converse directions, it must sink down through the second and third houses towards the lower meridian, and it cannot do this unless the earth reverses its rotation, a thing which never happens. [...]
>
> The first explanation is that, in forming such a direction as M.C. ☍ ♅, forces come into play that were in actual existence before the child's birth [...] and the effects signified by this are brought to fruition in the life history according to the usual measure of time.
>
> The second explanation is that the degree of R.A. that was on the cusp of the fourth house at birth, and therefore in opposition to the M.C., rises through the third, [second] and first houses until it reaches the mundane

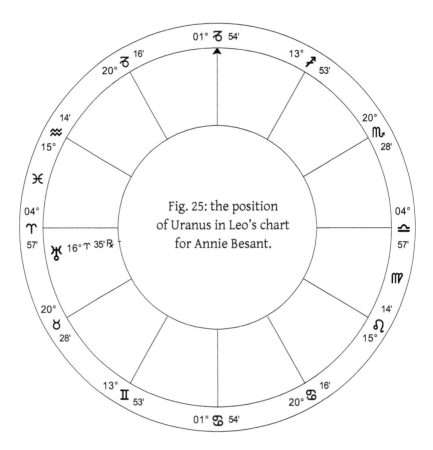

Fig. 25: the position
of Uranus in Leo's chart
for Annie Besant.

position that was occupied by Uranus at birth, so forming the direction M.C. ☌ ♅. This is accomplished by the eastward axial rotation of the earth after birth; and a similar explanation applies to other converse directions.[23]

In fact, while the arc required for bringing Uranus back to its prenatal opposition to the midheaven in Besant's chart, *against* the primary motion, is -76°32', the arc required for bringing the natal anti-culminating degree to the natal place of Uranus, *with* the primary motion, is 52°49'. The difference between the two methods thus amounts to more than 23 years![24]

As a result of the great popularity – even on the Continent – of Leo and a handful of other early 20th century English authors, the traditional meaning of the term *converse* was soon forgotten, and the new interpretation was projected onto older texts by successive generations of astrologers.

SUMMARY

❖ Innovations from the 17th century onwards have greatly increased the number of directions which can be formed in a nativity. One of these developments is the inclusion of newly-discovered planets and other bodies; another is the great number of new aspects invented.

❖ Apart from new zodiacal aspects, Placidus and his followers also added *mundane* 'aspects' as well as mundane and rapt *parallels*, all these being relationships based on the semi-arcs of the planets.

❖ Placidus further invented a directional method based on planetary poles and circles of position, meant to approximate the Ptolemaic method. Many later authors mistakenly accepted this approximation as the preferred method of Placidus.

❖ Placidus' belief that planetary influence was transmitted through light led him to advocate special directional methods when the Sun should happen to be below the horizon, in the *crepuscular* and *obscure arcs*, although these methods have rarely been used by later astrologers.

❖ Placidus also espoused a new definition of the Part of Fortune as a mundane point outside the zodiac, though still dependent on the positions of the Sun and Moon.

❖ In the late 19th or early 20th century, a few English authors began to use the term *converse directions* in the novel sense of 'directions against the primary motion', and its original meaning was gradually forgotten.

REFERENCES

1. See Holden 2008a:14 ff.
2. See Cooper [1814] 2004:79.
3. Lilly 1659:511 explicitly refers to the usefulness of these aspects in directions.
4. Schmidt 1993:17 ff. A footnote by Robert Hand states: 'This section actually describes *in mundo* aspects of exactly the kind that Placidus made so much use of in his primary directions. The math is different but the end result is nearly the same.' Actually, as we shall see, Placidean aspects *in mundo* are based on the same principles of proportional semi-arcs as the Ptolemaic system of directions, *not* on oblique ascensions, and the results are very different.
5. Robbins 1940:283. I have bracketed the words only implied in the original Greek.
6. Placidus even tried to establish Ptolemaic authority for this new definition of aspects by arguing (Cooper [1814] 2004:15 f) that as Venus cannot be more than 48° distant from the Sun in the zodiac, Ptolemy, speaking of a sextile between the two, must have meant a 'mundane' sextile. In reality, of course, Ptolemy was referring to whole-sign aspects.
7. Placidus' refusal to accept zodiacal aspects to the angles derived from his Aristotelian view of celestial mechanics, according to which only the primary motion from east to west is real, and the apparent secondary motion of the planets through the zodiac in the opposite direction is due to their various spheres moving less rapidly than the sphere containing the zodiac. The only real progress of the planets towards the angles or intermediate house cusps therefore takes place *in mundo*, and must be measured by mundane aspects.
8. See Holden 2008b:81 ff; Cooper [1814] 2004:19 f, 53.
9. Pearce [1911] 2006:194.
10. For instances of the former see Oxley 1830:138 ff; Wilson [1819] 2006:397 f. The crepuscular and obscure arcs are present in Bishop & Kirby 1687, but absent from Partridge 1697 and from most later authors, including Worsdale 1828. Pearce [1911] 2006:194 states: 'The "crepusculine" and "obscure" arcs of Placidus and Wilson should be disregarded. The *semi-arc* method is the true motion in Nature.'
11. Holden 1994:64.

12. Cooper [1814] 2004:308. Wilson [1819] 2006:305 f, rejecting the concept of the Part entirely, sees in this statement a strong proof of astrology: '[Placidus] could find truth in the planetary configurations, because their effects are founded on the immutable laws of nature, but when he came to investigate the effects of the ⊕ he could "find no truth in it," because there was none.'

13. See Robbins 1940:274 ff.

14. Formulae for calculating the mundane Part of Fortune according to Negusanti and Placidus are found in Appendix I.

15. Nevertheless, it is of course possible to project the mundane Part of Fortune, however distant, onto the ecliptic; cf. Oxley 1830:156.

16. Although an artificial semi-arc may be assigned to the mundane Part of Fortune in order to determine its house position (cf. Appendix I), the Part does not in fact describe such an arc by its diurnal motion. Sepharial [1915] 2006:67 fails to understand this astronomical reality. Placidus himself wrote: '[A]s it may very reasonably be doubted whether the ⊕ institutes the directions by converse motion [i.e., by its own diurnal motion], I will omit speaking of this till another time, and, in the interim, see what experience says.'

17. A planet in parallel of declination with Placidus' mundane Part of Fortune will therefore always be simultaneously in parallel with the Moon, which, as pointed out by Wilson [1819] 2006:306, makes it difficult to establish the relative importance of the two. Worsdale 1828:16 ff, 128 ff presents a variant mode of calculating the mundane Part (although his example calculation on p. 17 appears to be flawed), stating that '[n]othing can be more absurd than allowing it to claim the same Latitude and Declination as the Moon'. (Placidus had in fact claimed only the Moon's declination for the Part, not its latitude.) Worsdale's method is to compute the oblique ascensions or descensions of the Sun and Moon under their respective Placidean poles and project the distance from the eastern horizon along the celestial equator. The point reached is the oblique ascension or descension of the Part of Fortune, which is then reassigned to the ecliptic and given the right ascension and declination of its ecliptical degree, despite Worsdale's assertion that it 'can only be directed in Mundo'. For an explanation of technical terms, see Appendix I and the Glossary.

18. Partridge 1697:44 f. Partridge refers particularly to one place in *Astrologia Gallica* 22 (translated in Holden 1994:53 ff), but there are several such

examples in Morin's work, including one at the end of Book 17 (Holden 2008b:115). Lilly and other 17th century authors went one step further and began directing the zodiacal degrees natally on the cusps of the 2nd, 3rd and 4th houses to the horizon (see, for instance, Lilly 1659:665 f) – something Morin would not have countenanced.

19. Abenragel 1551:160.

20. Wilson [1819] 2006:20.

21. See Oxley 1830:64; Worsdale 1828:20 ff *et passim*.

22. Leo 1923:297 f; additions in square brackets mine. The same use of 'direct' and 'converse' can be found in Pearce [1911] 2006:182 ff; Sepharial [1915] 2006:29 ff *et passim*. Worsdale 1828:vii in his usual manner attacks Thomas White's *The Celestial Intelligencer* as 'a wretched compilation of borrowed, and stolen trash, collected from most of the pirates I have mentioned [...] he has given the most inconsistent examples to prove, that the Planets, after they have passed the Ascendant and Midheaven, return back, contrary to the regular order of nature, and the distance of the Stars from those Angles, he is pleased to stile Arcs of Directions [...]'. This could possibly refer to an early doctrine of directions against the primary motion; but I have so far been unable to find in White 1810 the unnatural arcs to which Worsdale objects.

23. Leo 1923:296.

24. Gauricus 1557:84 contains one example which is likely to be a similar error or approximation, although it might possibly be a very early and isolated instance of intentional directing against the primary motion. This is the chart from ar-Rijāl discussed above (see note 19), but with degrees entered for the ascendant (22° Leo) and Moon (30° Cancer), as well as for the midheaven and other house cusps (in the Regiomontanus system, and calculated for the vicinity of Rome rather than for ar-Rijāl's location in what is now Tunisia). Gaurico subtracts the oblique ascension of the Moon from that of the ascendant, against the primary motion, obtaining an arc of 28°21′ corresponding to 28y 4m 6d. He remarks: '☽ in ♋ with a nebulous star in the 12th. When it arrived at the ascendant, it made the native blind in the left eye.' Gaurico's timing of the event bears no relation to ar-Rijāl's, and it is not clear from where he takes his additional information, unless he manufactured it. I am grateful to Rumen Kolev for bringing the treatment of this chart by ar-Rijāl and Gaurico to my attention.

9

The Hyleg and the Length of Life

The earliest purpose of primary directions seems to have been to determine the length of a native's life. Although ancient and classical authors from the 1st century onwards have used the technique to predict other types of events as well, it has retained a strong link with the prognostication of death. Certainly this has always been one of its most important uses. In a phrase perhaps originating with Nechepso-Petosiris, and echoed by astrologers throughout the centuries, Ptolemy writes:

> The consideration of the length of life takes the leading place among inquiries about events following birth, for, as the ancient says, it is ridiculous to attach particular predictions to one who, by the constitution of the years of his life, will never attain at all to the time of the predicted events.[1]

The 'constitution of the years of life' is found by the primary directions involving the main significator of life. This significator may be a luminary, planet, or other chart point, chosen according to particular rules. From medieval times it has been generally known as the *hyleg*.

Hyleg (with several variant spellings, such as *hylech, alhileg*, etc.) is a Medieval Latin form of Arabic *(al)-hīlāj*.[2] The Arabic word in its turn is derived from Middle Persian *hīlāk* 'releasing', a translation of the Greek word *aphetēs* (ἀφέτης) 'releaser, discharger' – used, for instance, of the starter in a race, and derived from the same verb as *aphesis* 'direction' (mentioned in Chapter 2).[3] The hyleg is also known, in a Latinized form of the Greek, as the *apheta*, or by a purely Latin word as the *prorogator* 'dispenser'. It is often referred to as the *lord, giver, significator* or *moderator* of life.

The hyleg, then, is conceived of as the starter of the course of life, a course described by the primary directions. The oldest preserved method of finding and directing the hyleg is given by Ptolemy in his *Tetrabiblos*. The method of Dorotheus, which seems to have differed in certain respects from that of Ptolemy, has not been preserved in the original Greek (cf. Chapter 2). Nor does the technique of primary directions, or the concept of hyleg, appear to have been part of that Hellenistic astrological lore which in the early centuries CE made its way into India.[4] The following account will be based chiefly on the precepts of Ptolemy.[5] We shall also examine the views of other classical and later authors from the Middle Ages to the modern era.

Ptolemy's rules for determining the hyleg

All authors agree that the hyleg is determined on the basis of *sect* or *hairesis* (αἵρεσις) – an all-important factor in ancient astrology.[6] Planets and, in this case, certain other points are divided into two sects or groups: the solar or diurnal (daytime) sect, and the lunar or nocturnal (nighttime) sect. In determining the hyleg according to Ptolemy, the following points are of relevance:

Diurnal points	*Nocturnal points*
The Sun	The Moon
The prenatal conjunction	The prenatal prevention
The ascendant	The Part of Fortune

The *prenatal conjunction* is the last conjunction of the Sun and Moon (i.e., the last New Moon) before birth, while the *prenatal prevention* is the last Full Moon before birth – in other words, the position of the Moon at the time of its exact opposition to the Sun.[7] Ptolemy, as discussed in the previous chapter, wants the Part of Fortune to function as a 'lunar ascendant', a point in the zodiac always as far away from the Moon as the ascendant is from the Sun. He therefore deviates from the standard Hellenistic practice of calculating this Part or Lot by different formulae for day and night births.

To find the hyleg, we begin by noting the *hylegiacal* (or *aphetical*) places, which are the ascendant and those houses above the horizon which are in aspect to the ascendant by sextile, square, trine or opposition. To Ptolemy, apparently using equal houses (at least in this context), this means – in descending order of strength – the 10th, 1st, 11th, 7th and 9th houses. Preference is thus given to the eastern side of the chart (where planets rise) over the western (where they set), and to angular and succedent houses over cadent ones.

In a daytime birth, when the Sun is found above the horizon, Ptolemy tells us to seek the hyleg from among the following points:

1.   The Sun, if it is found in a hylegiacal place.
2.   If it is not, then the Moon, if found in a hylegiacal place.
3.   If it is not, then the strongest planet which is in a hylegiacal place and has at least *three* kinds of dignity in any *one* of the diurnal points above. Dignity may be of five kinds:
      a) domicile;
      b) exaltation;
      c) triplicity;
      d) terms;
      e) aspect (reckoned from sign to sign, and presumably including conjunctions).
4.   If no such planet is found, the ascendant itself will be hyleg.

Similarly, in a nighttime birth (with the Sun below the horizon), the hyleg is found by choosing:

1.   The Moon, if it is found in a hylegiacal place.
2.   If it is not, then the Sun, if found in a hylegiacal place. (This can only be in the 1st house, or just below the horizon in the west – Ptolemy allows a 5° orb for the 7th house cusp.)
3.   If it is not, then the strongest planet which is in a hylegiacal place and has at least three kinds of dignity in any one of the nocturnal points above.
4.   If no such planet is found, and the birth was preceded by a Full Moon (a *preventional* birth), the Part of Fortune will be hyleg. Some manuscripts of Ptolemy's text identify the ascendant as the final option if the Part is not in a hylegiacal place.
5.   If the birth was preceded by a New Moon (a *conjunctional* birth), the ascendant will be hyleg.

Having listed these fairly mechanical rules, Ptolemy goes on to modify them slightly: if both luminaries, or a luminary and the 'ruler of the sect' (a planet qualified as above) should happen to be in hylegiacal places, we should take the one in the stronger place.[8] When both luminaries are in hylegiacal places, a third planet should be preferred only if it occupies a hylegiacal place stronger than those of both luminaries *and* has dignity in both sects.

Finding the killing point

Once the hyleg has been determined, the next task is to identify the planet or point which will end the course of life. This is known in Greek as the *anairetēs* (ἀναιρέτης) 'destroyer, murderer' (often Latinized as *anaereta* or, less correctly, *anareta*), or by a purely Latin word as the *abscissor* 'cutter-off'. It is also referred to as the *interfector* or interficient point, from Latin *interficio* 'destroy, kill, slay'. We shall refer to it as the anaereta.

In his rules for determining the anaereta, Ptolemy makes a distinction between two types of nativities. When the hyleg is found in the eastern or left-hand side of the chart, Ptolemy seeks the anaereta only from the malefic planets and their aspects approaching the hyleg by the primary motion. In other words, he allows only *direct* directions in the traditional sense of the term (cf. Chapter 1). The main anaeretas are Saturn and Mars, who kill both by bodily conjunction and by aspect – particularly by square and opposition. As mentioned in the previous chapter, Ptolemy also allows sextiles of long ascension or trines of short ascension to end life, as well as sextiles between signs 'beholding' each other.[9] Apart from Saturn and Mars, Mercury becomes malefic by being configured with them (by conjunction or aspect); and when the Moon is hyleg, the 'place of the Sun' can destroy life (Ptolemy does not explicitly mention aspects of the Sun).

In all of these cases, however, the potential anaereta is prevented from killing if located in benefic terms (bounds) or aspected by either of the two benefics – Ptolemy says by square, trine or opposition, but omits the sextile, perhaps by oversight. The anaereta should be within 12° of the aspect of Jupiter, or 8° of that of Venus, for these aspects to save.[10] Likewise, in a bodily conjunction, a potential anaereta with a different latitude (north or south) than that of the hyleg will not kill. When several directions to the hyleg are active, some benefic and others malefic, the astrologer must determine which side is stronger, and particularly whether any of the planets involved are in their heliacal setting or rising – in other words, entering or leaving combustion; for Ptolemy does not allow any planet under the rays of the Sun the power either to destroy or to save.

The symbolism of setting

When the hyleg is found in the western or right-hand side of the chart, between the midheaven and the descendant, Ptolemy allows two methods of direction. One is directing the malefics and their aspects to the hyleg by direct motion as just described. The other is directing the hyleg by its own primary motion to its setting point on the western horizon or descendant, which becomes the killing point 'by causing the lord of life to vanish'. This echoes earlier doctrines discussed by Ptolemy's contemporary, Vettius Valens (cf. below). Traditionally, such a direction would be labelled converse.

On its way towards the descendant, the hyleg will typically pass the conjunctions or aspects of other planets. Ptolemy considers these aspects to be less effective because they do not take the pursuing role. For this reason they do not kill, but they do modify the number of years indicated by the hyleg's arc of direction to the descendant.

According to Ptolemy, the aspecting malefics (Saturn and Mars) subtract years, while the benefics (Jupiter and Venus) add years; once again, Mercury becomes malefic or benefic by its configurations with the other planets. The number of years assigned to each planet is based on its *horary* (or *hourly*) *times*, or rather on the horary times of its zodiacal degree. The horary times of any point comprise one twelfth of its diurnal or nocturnal arc – the time it spends above or below the horizon – measured in degrees of right ascension. The diurnal arc is used for a day birth, the nocturnal for a night birth.

Thus, if a planet's point of longitude, at the place of birth, remains above the horizon for exactly 16 hours of clock time each day, its diurnal horary times will be 16h/12 = 1h 20m, or 80 minutes of clock time. As each degree of right ascension corresponds to just under 4 minutes of time, the diurnal horary times expressed in such degrees would be just over 20°, corresponding to some 20 years of life. The same zodiacal point would then remain below the horizon for 8 hours every day, making its nocturnal horary times 8h/12 = 0h 40m, which is to say 40/4 = 10° of right ascension, corresponding to 10 years.

However, a planet will only give or take away the full number of its years if it is exactly conjunct the ascendant; and if it should be conjunct the descendant, it will neither give nor take away anything at all. Planets located between these two points will give or take away years by proportion. Thus, a planet located in a zodiacal degree which had passed exactly one third of its diurnal arc from ascendant to descendant would give or take away two thirds of the years represented by its horary times. If the planet were Jupiter and its horary times 20, Jupiter would therefore add 13.33

years of life to those indicated by the arc of direction between the hyleg and the descendant.[11] This rather involved method does not seem to have been much used in practice.

The quality of death

According to Ptolemy, not only the time, but even the quality and circumstances of death are to be judged from the anaereta, whether this be the descendant, a planet, or a place of aspect. The kind of death will correspond to the planets occupying the anaeretical places; or, if no planets should be in these places, to 'those first being carried to them' by the primary motion. In other words, if no planet is conjunct the anaereta, the directions immediately following will indicate the nature of death. Complexity is increased by other planets in aspect, as well as by the individual natures of the zodiacal signs and the terms occupied by the anaereta.

Ptolemy gives a detailed list of the illnesses by which each of the five planets (excluding the luminaries) may cause the native's death, from rheumatism and pneumonia to madness and melancholy. This list holds good as long as the planet in question is not unduly afflicted; but if both malefics should afflict the anaeretic place by conjunction, square, or opposition, or if one or both of them should afflict one or both of the luminaries, the native dies a violent and remarkable death. Ptolemy's list of possible causes includes fighting wild animals on festival days, being shipwrecked or killed by pirates, crushed by a collapsing building, burnt alive, or crucified. Here, too, the details depend on several factors, including aspects, zodiacal signs and particular fixed stars.

Practical considerations: two examples
Do Ptolemy's methods of selecting and directing the hyleg hold up in practice? My personal, tentative conclusion is that his first method is fundamentally correct but that converse directions (in the traditional sense of bringing the hyleg *with* the primary motion to the planets and their aspects) need to be given equal weight with direct directions (bringing the planets and their aspects with the primary motion to the hyleg). I also find Ptolemy's three-dignity rule somewhat doubtful – particularly as I am less than satisfied with the usefulness of term and triplicity rulerships, both of which exist in more than one version – and the Part of Fortune even more so.

While determining the hyleg and anaereta can sometimes be a straightforward affair, it is often complicated by such factors as choice of zodiac and house system. Changing from equal or whole-sign houses to a quadrant-based division, or from one quadrant system to another, may cause the luminaries and other planets to move into or out of the hylegiacal houses. Equally, a change of zodiac could grant or remove the dignities required for a planet to become hyleg. My own preference is for a sidereal zodiac and quadrant (Alcabitius) houses, and I do believe that the relative strength of oriental and angular houses over the occidental and cadent is important – the 9th being the weakest of all hylegiacal places. In figure 26, the Sun is just outside the cusp of the 9th house; other quadrant systems (Porphyry, Campanus, Regiomontanus, Placidus) would push it further into the 8th. By contrast, whole-sign and equal houses would place the Sun squarely in the 9th house, even rather close to the 10th cusp. In the latter systems, the Sun would be the natural choice for hyleg, as the

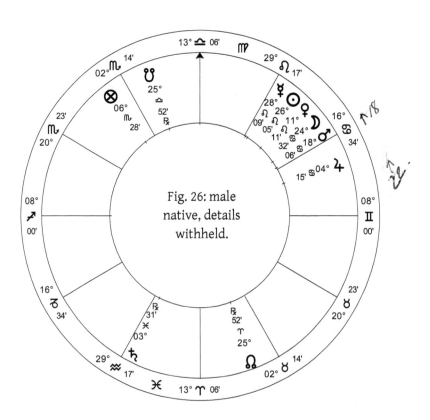

Fig. 26: male native, details withheld.

nativity is a diurnal one (the Sun being above the horizon) and the 9th is a hylegiacal place. In the quadrant house systems, however, the Sun would be less fit to be hyleg.

If the Sun is discounted as hyleg, the next candidate is the Moon, which is in the 8th house (and therefore disqualified) by all systems except Campanus. No other planet possesses the dignities required for becoming hyleg. The final option is the ascendant.

At the age of 33y 9m, the native was killed in a vehicle accident. There were no evil directions to either of the luminaries around this time – the Sun, indeed, was actually conjunct Jupiter. The ascendant, however, was afflicted by the opposition of Mars, a first-rate anaereta and most appropriate considering the kind of death. Mars is also located in the 8th house, conjunct the cusp. The arc of direction for the given time of birth was 32°42' for an opposition *in zodiaco*, or 34°37' *in mundo*. An adjustment of the birth time by a few minutes either way would make one or the other of these two directions near-exact at the time of death, using Ptolemy's key of 1 degree per year (cf. Chapter 6).

Figure 27 is another diurnal nativity, and one in which the Sun is undoubtedly hylegiacal according to all house systems except equal houses (where it falls in the 8th) and possibly Campanus (which puts it partilely on the 9th cusp for the given birth time). But while the Sun occupies the weakest of hylegiacal places, Mars is found in one of the strongest. Does Mars have the required three dignities? We see that it does: it rules the ascendant by term, domicile, and conjunction. Mars therefore takes precedence over the Sun and becomes hyleg.

At the age of 37y 4m, the native died from a chronic lung disease. Again, there were no particularly evil directions to the Sun around this time; in this case too, the Sun was in fact approaching a conjunction with Jupiter. But Saturn, having recently set at the western horizon, perfected an opposition to Mars *in mundo* with an arc of 37°39'.

Other classical views

Ptolemy's rules were formulated against a background of existing opinions and theories. His junior contemporary Vettius Valens, in criticizing certain anonymous predecessors, gives us some idea of their way of thinking:

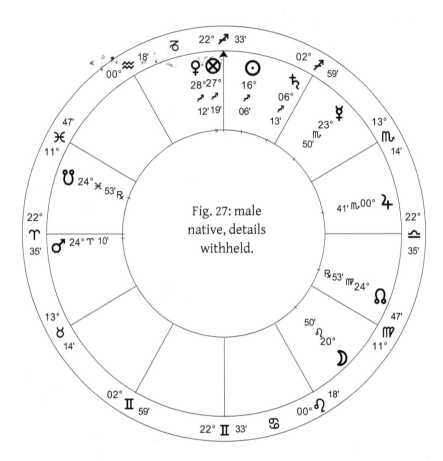

Fig. 27: male native, details withheld.

As some, out of envy or ignorance, treat of the direction only one-sidedly and obscurely (for they appear always to use the extent of degrees from the aphetic degree up to the side of the square, according to the ascensions), it is necessary for us to explain the distinctions further. For we find both nativities which have passed over the side of the square – and especially in the signs of short ascension, despite the ancient strictly asserting this to be impossible – and again, without the malefics casting their rays, nativities not having completed the square.[12]

The square or quarter-circle seems to have been fundamental to some early theories on the length of life. Dividing the 360° of the zodiac by four, with some variation to either side depending on the rising times of the various signs, gives a reasonable approximation of the years of a full human life-span. The aphetic or hylegiacal degree – the degree of the Sun, Moon or ascendant, or even of the midheaven – reaching the end of its square would indicate the native's maximum life-span, which could then be curtailed by malefic conjunctions or aspects. Vettius argues that mundane quadrants (formed by the four angles of the chart) rather than zodiacal squares should be used for this purpose.

Vettius also places great importance on the ruler of the terms occupied by the hyleg, and on whether or not this ruler aspects the hyleg.[13] His methods of finding the length of life, which are obscure in spite of a number of examples meant to illustrate them, make use of symbolic numbers of years assigned to the term ruler.[14] The most fully worked-out example is as follows (fig. 28):[15]

The Moon in the midheaven is apheta or hyleg, located in the terms of Mercury (also, as it happens, term ruler of the ascendant), whose full years are 76. Vettius divides these 76 years by the 12 parts or 'hours' of Mercury's diurnal arc, making 6y 4m for each such hour. He then tries to determine the elapsed portion of these hours, not by rising times, but from the 35 zodiacal degrees between Mercury and the ascendant. These 35° are equated with 2 1/3 hours (properly corresponding to 35° of *right ascension*), making a total of 2 1/3 × 6y 4m = 14y 9m 10d. Subtracting this from Mercury's 76 years leaves a life expectancy of 61y 2m 20d according to the term ruler of the hyleg.

Vettius then measures the distance from the ascendant to the Moon, this time according to the approximate rising times of the signs: 40 for Libra, 36 for Scorpio, and 32 for Sagittarius. The 22° remaining of Libra give 22/30 × 40 years; the whole of Scorpio, 36 years; and the first 17° of Sagittarius, 17/30 × 32 years: in all, 83y 5m 18d. This is the longevity given by the Moon, unless a destroying planet should cast its aspect somewhere in between the ascendant and the Moon (and it is difficult to see how it could avoid doing so). In such a case, the native may live only until the Moon reaches the malefic aspect, or up to the end of the 61 years granted by Mercury, whichever comes first.

There is certainly a loose, improvisational quality about this process, as well as a none too firm grasp on astronomical fundamentals, and perhaps Ptolemy cannot be blamed for wishing to put it on a more rational footing. His second method discussed above is obviously derived from the same elements as that of Vettius: the quadrant between midheaven and descendant representing the span of life, with the planets adding and subtracting years based on their hourly times. In all probability, however,

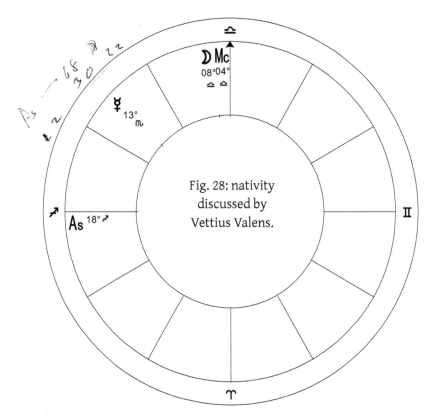

Fig. 28: nativity
discussed by
Vettius Valens.

Ptolemy's second method was a wholly theoretical construct, and few later astrologers seem to have adopted it.

An even earlier author was Balbillus, who lived in the 1st century CE and, like his father Thrasyllus before him, served as a Roman imperial astrologer. Two birth charts discussed by Balbillus in connection with the length of life were preserved in a late Byzantine text; the earlier of these can be dated to 21 January, 72 BCE.[16]

Balbillus' treatment of this chart is of particular interest because he rejects the Sun, Moon and ascendant, and instead selects Saturn as apheta or hyleg. Such preferring of another planet over a mere point such as the ascendant, Part of Fortune or prenatal syzygy agrees with the procedure used by Ptolemy. In this diurnal chart, Saturn rules the Sun by terms and domicile; they are also conjunct by sign. Whether Saturn could be regarded as angular would depend on the house division used and on the exact degree of the ascendant.[17]

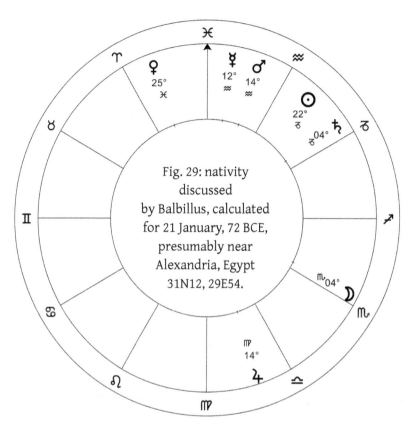

Fig. 29: nativity
discussed
by Balbillus, calculated
for 21 January, 72 BCE,
presumably near
Alexandria, Egypt
31N12, 29E54.

The whole-sign house division shown here was not necessarily used by Balbillus.

Balbillus takes Mars to be the anaereta and directs it to Saturn to find
the length of life. Unfortunately, he does not tell us how long that would
be.[18] We therefore have no means of knowing whether Balbillus used a
simple method of rising times like Vettius Valens, or a more astronomically
sophisticated method like that of Ptolemy.

Medieval developments and the alcochoden

During late antiquity and the Middle Ages, the determination and directions
of the hyleg were taken up by numerous authors, with many variations.
The rules given by these authors are a mixture of Ptolemy, pre-Ptolemaic
Hellenistic material, and later innovations; and it is not always possible to
distinguish between the two latter categories. Taking the Ptolemaic rules

as our starting-point, we may note that later authors tend to differ from them in three major respects.

First, they increase the number of hylegiacal places to include houses below the horizon – the 2nd, 4th, 5th and sometimes, for the Moon, the 3rd (its house of 'rejoicing') – as well as the 8th house. The latter is particularly surprising in view of the fact that these authors typically look to the 8th house for the native's death, something Ptolemy does not do. They also require that the Sun occupy a masculine sign in order to be hyleg when found in the 'feminine quarters' between the upper midheaven and descendant or between the lower midheaven and ascendant, and some similarly insist on a feminine sign for the Moon when found between the ascendant and midheaven. Not all accept the 9th house as hylegiacal.

Second, most later authors do not use planets other than the luminaries as hyleg, but instead add another point: the prenatal lunation or syzygy (*syzygia ante nativitatem*) – that is to say, the degree of the New Moon ('conjunction') or Full Moon ('prevention') most recently preceding birth.[19] There is some disagreement over which degree to use for the Full Moon: that of the Moon or that of the Sun. They also increase the number of potential anaeretas to include, among other points, the lunar nodes and certain fixed stars.[20]

Third, these authors insist that no planet or point can become hyleg without being aspected by at least one of its rulers or dispositors. As seen above, this teaching goes back to Hellenistic times; but to the Hellenistic rulerships of terms, domicile, exaltation and triplicity most later authors add a fifth, that of *decan* or *face*.[21] Some appear for this purpose to regard planetary antiscia (cf. Chapter 8) as a species of aspect. As a point not aspected by a ruler can never be hyleg, it is possible, according to the medieval writers, for a nativity to be entirely without a hyleg. Naturally, this is not considered to bode well for the native's longevity.

The ruler aspecting the hyleg acquired a particular significance in medieval astrology, where it became known as *alcochoden*. The word is a Latinized form of the Perso-Arabic *al-kadḥudāh*, which in turn translates the Greek *oikodespotēs* (οἰκοδεσπότης) 'master of the house'.[22] Just as the hyleg was known as the 'giver of life', the alcochoden became known as the 'giver of years', and the method of predicting the length of life shifted in emphasis from primary directions as such into a complex and sometimes jumbled system of additions and subtractions.

To the challenge of determining the correct hyleg was added the problem of then selecting the right alcochoden from up to five potential candidates. Next, the strength of this alcochoden had to be gauged in order to ascertain whether it would grant its greater, middle or lesser years (see Appendix III) – or, in extreme cases, only the corresponding number of months or days of life. A rough rule of thumb stated that an angular planet would give its greater years; a succedent planet, its middle years; and a cadent planet, its lesser years; but there were many exceptions and special considerations. Finally, each planet aspecting the alcochoden had to be similarly evaluated in order to decide whether it would add to or subtract from the span of life indicated, and if so, by how much. Opinions abounded, and no two authors seem wholly to agree. In this process, the directions of the hyleg played the relatively minor role of confirming or slightly modifying the time of death indicated by the alcochoden.

The neo-Ptolemaic renaissance

As discussed in Chapter 2, the Renaissance saw a desire among many astrologers to return to classical, pre-Arabic sources, in keeping with the general idealization of classical culture at the time. In practice, this meant a return to Ptolemy, Arabic translations of whose *Tetrabiblos* had been retranslated into Latin as the *Quadripartite* and preserved when many other works were lost. In this way Ptolemy's work gained an authority beyond anything it had enjoyed during the classical period.

In the 17th century, two of the astrologers most devoted to restoring their art to its imagined pristine purity – Jean-Baptiste Morin and Placidus – reached very different points of view on the subject of the hyleg. Morin simply did away with the concept, treating the question of life-span like any other under his general principles of chart interpretation. The discussion of the nativity of King Gustav II Adolf of Sweden (known in Latin as Gustavus Adolphus), to which Morin frequently returns in his *Astrologia Gallica*, illustrates his approach.

Despite his own devout Catholicism, Morin was highly impressed with the Protestant monarch, calling him 'magnanimous and unconquerable [...] a prince very worthy of a Christian empire, if he had only been a Catholic' – perhaps a rather strange epitaph for a man who had spent the better part of his life waging war against Catholics.[23] Morin also claimed to have predicted the King's violent death to Cardinal Richelieu: 'not in fact on the very time when it happened, but a little later on account of the false moment of his birth hour that was given to me'.[24] He subsequently rectified the King's time of birth by this event, adding five minutes to the given time. This adjustment would have altered the relevant directions by approximately 1y 3m.

Which directions, then, prompted Morin to make his prediction? In his own words,

> the MC was coming by direction to the square of Jupiter and Saturn, immediately and as closely following with the body of Mars afflicted in the MC. They were signifying the greatest misfortune in undertakings and battles and also a violent death, as I had predicted [...] And that occurrence of three anaeretas was horrendous![25]

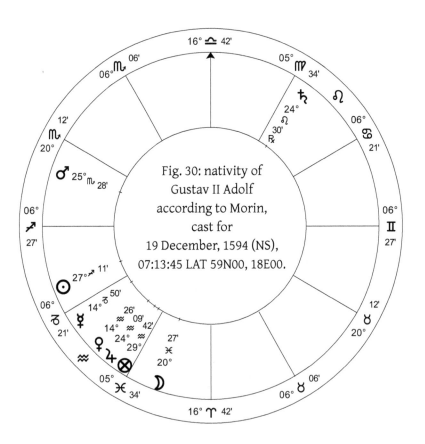

Fig. 30: nativity of Gustav II Adolf according to Morin, cast for 19 December, 1594 (NS), 07:13:45 LAT 59N00, 18E00.

Not only Saturn and Mars, but Jupiter too becomes a killer in Morin's view. Being the exaltation ruler of the sign on the 8th house cusp – the house of death – Jupiter will harm especially by its evil aspects, and even more so as it is afflicted by both the malefics, and as its own ruler Saturn is afflicted in the 8th house itself. Morin continues:

> Moreover, a public and famous death was being signified on account of the Sun, ruler of the 8th, in the 1st; and the death was from a fired piece of lead on account of Saturn in the fire sign Leo, and then from iron on account of Mars.[26]

Here rulership of the 8th house is assigned to the Sun, whose sign Leo is intercepted in that house and occupied by Saturn.

Morin was aware that others would object to using directions to the midheaven for predictions of death, as the midheaven was neither a significator of life in his own system nor one of Ptolemy's possible hylegs (although it had been used as hyleg by other classical authors). In his defence, he argued that while the ascendant signifies life generally, a death caused by the native's own actions (such as warfare), which are the domain of the midheaven, could properly be predicted by directions to that point.

In contrast to Morin, Placidus viewed Ptolemy's text as gospel truth – albeit a gospel which could be subjected to a most implausible exegesis in order to save his own notions of an astrology conformable to nature and reason. His treatment of the chart of Gustav II Adolf is very different from Morin's, and illustrates several of his innovations.

Placidus mentions slight variations on the King's time of birth, adopting one half an hour later than the time used by Morin but adding that 'however it be, it matters not, as we do not direct the horoscope [i.e., ascendant], but the ☉'.[27] As the Sun is in the 1st house while the Moon (ruler of the sect) is further below the horizon, the Sun is the obvious hyleg by Ptolemy's rules. Placidus, noting the same configuration of Saturn, Mars and Jupiter as discussed above, goes on to direct Jupiter to the Sun (a direct direction) as well as the Sun to Mars (a converse direction in the traditional sense). Unlike Morin, he does not regard Jupiter as an anaereta, but argues – like Ptolemy – that Jupiter on its own is helpless against both the malefics.

As the Sun is in the 'crepuscular arcs' (cf. Chapter 8), Placidus directs Jupiter, and the opposition of Saturn, to the Sun's circle of altitude parallel to the horizon. This somewhat laborious process yields an arc of direction of 41°21′. In accordance with his own key for equating degrees of arc with years of life (cf. Chapter 6), Placidus adds this figure to the right ascension of the Sun in the King's nativity, 266°59′, the result of which is 308°20′. By its secondary motion along the zodiac, the Sun reached 308°20′ of right ascension just over 38 days after birth; Placidus therefore considers the direction to have been perfected at the age of 38 years. Gustav II Adolf was killed in battle at the age of 37y 11m.[28]

Placidus also directs the Sun to the body of Mars above the horizon, approximating the arc of direction with the help of poles to 39°36′ (within half a degree of the Ptolemaic value). He then calculates the direction of the Sun to the *mundane* square of Saturn at 42°03′, and to its mundane parallel at 43°17′. All these directions are converse in the older sense of the word, as they involve moving the significator (hyleg) along its own diurnal circle. Together they form what is often called 'a train of directions' to the hyleg.

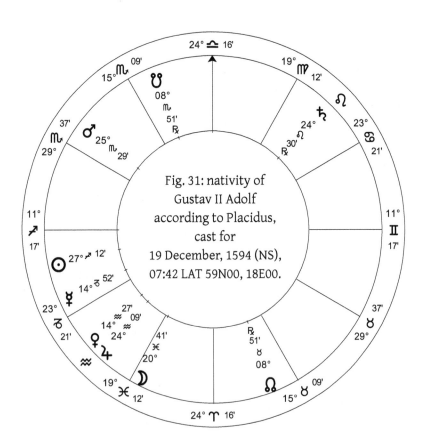

Fig. 31: nativity of Gustav II Adolf according to Placidus, cast for 19 December, 1594 (NS), 07:42 LAT 59N00, 18E00.

The battery of techniques worked out by Placidus, which was adopted by technical-minded British astrologers in the 17th century and continued in use into the 19th, produces an almost overwhelming number of directions. Its followers therefore tend not to view individual directions in isolation, but rather to look for such trains of direction. John Worsdale, who devoted much time to predicting what he called 'personal dissolution', states that in a train of malefic directions to the hyleg, the first direction generally gives the *time* of death, while those following indicate the circumstances.[29] But there are exceptions:

> for it sometimes happens, that when the giver of Life has arrived at the *first Direction* in the beginning of those hostile primary Motions, which threaten dissolution, Life is preserved by other benign Rays, Orbs, and Terms, in which the Prorogator, assuming the powerful Aphetical Dignity, is surrounded in the Zodiac, and in Mundo [...] but when the giver of Life arrives at the *next* Malefic Direction in the train, then Death will ensue [...][30]

Finally, two malefic directions to the hyleg occurring in succession, 'even when they are far remote', will always kill the native unless there is 'sufficient benign aid' from unafflicted benefics.[31]

A look at one of Worsdale's example charts will give an idea of his style of work. Samuel Portwood was a farmer's son from the village of Donington, not far from Worsdale's residence in Lincoln. The young man had taught himself some astrology with the help of books borrowed from Worsdale himself, and took an optimistic view both of his own chart and of his future prospects – an attitude which Worsdale endeavoured to correct:

> I told him that all his observations were founded on error, as other Astral Causes of a different nature, were the Auxiliaries of his success, which would continue but a *short time* [...] I also informed him that though he had many Books, Papers, and documents of *mine* in his possession, which I expected he would peruse to the time of his Death, yet there was one that surpassed all others, on which the following words were written.—"*Prepare to meet thy God, for soon thou shalt surely Die.*"[32]

Portwood's nativity was a diurnal one, with the Sun in the 11th Placidean house. He therefore considered the Sun to be his hyleg, but Worsdale disagreed: 'because that Luminary had not arrived at that part of the Eleventh, where he claims his full, and perfect Hylegiacal Dignity'.[33] This is another doctrine of Placidus': although the 11th is a hylegiacal place, the hyleg must be at least halfway between rising and culminating – that is, above the horizon by at least half of its diurnal semi-arc.[34] But the warning, given in October, 1821, was not heeded:

> [...] though he had obtained MY DOCUMENTS which showed that the *King of Terrors*, was nearly at the Door of his dwelling, to execute his final summons, yet he would not be convinced that the Moon was Hyleg, strictly, and absurdly depending on the Sun as the right prorogator, which he vainly believed, promised him Health, and old Age [...][35]

Worsdale argued tersely that the luminaries and ascendant being afflicted, and their rulers not dignified, 'show Life, and every object desirable, to be of short duration'. It is easy to see that the Moon is afflicted by its close conjunction with Saturn (though their latitudes differ); and that this also affects the ascendant in Cancer ruled by the Moon. The affliction to the Sun is less clear. Possibly Worsdale had the wide and separating square from Mars in mind, although there is also an applying (and somewhat closer) sextile to Jupiter.

Mars and Mercury, rulers of the luminaries, are both cadent, and not in their domiciles or exaltations. The Part of Fortune, the last potential hyleg, is ruled by Venus, which is angular, in its domicile, and – in Worsdale's view – aspected by Jupiter (apparently by an out-of-sign trine). Without it, he states, 'the Native would have been involved in great troubles, and misfortunes'. But this saving grace was not enough: the true hyleg remained afflicted, and Worsdale did not believe it could withstand the direction to the rapt parallel of the Sun (which, with Ptolemy, he considered an anaereta when the Moon is hyleg) occurring at the age of 34y 3m.

This fateful direction is followed in Worsdale's list by several other directions to the Moon, due to perfect over the next five years: to the mundane square of Jupiter, the mundane sextile of Venus, the zodiacal semi-sextile of Saturn, and the mundane square of the Sun. Although the list of promissors contains both the benefics, Worsdale comments that 'they could not save, owing to the Terms of the Enemies [i.e., malefics] being united near the Anaeretical places', and that 'their apparent benign power became null, and void, because they were both afflicted with the same Directions of Saturn in the World, and by Mars also in the subsequent Motions'.[36] Samuel Portwood died on 16 October, 1824, at the age of 34y 4m.

As we have seen, the neo-Ptolemaic method of Placidus and his followers contains much that differs both from Ptolemy and from the

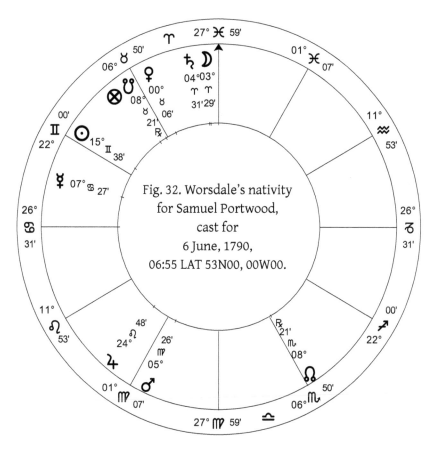

Fig. 32. Worsdale's nativity
for Samuel Portwood,
cast for
6 June, 1790,
06:55 LAT 53N00, 00W00.

greater astrological tradition. From personal experience I would vouch for the principle of mundane squares to the angles – in other words, that a planet conjunct the upper or lower midheaven has an impact on the ascendant and descendant as well. This principle probably extends to planets closely conjunct the angles; but I have found nothing to support the rest of Placidus' mundane aspects.

Example: the murder of a minister
As a final exercise in this ancient and complex branch of primary directions, let us examine the nativity of the late Anna Lindh, Swedish Minister for Foreign Affairs, who was stabbed to death in her 47th year. Although such considerations would not have been regarded by Ptolemy, the ruler of the ascendant in the 8th house, squared by the ruler of the 8th, is a strong testimony of premature death.

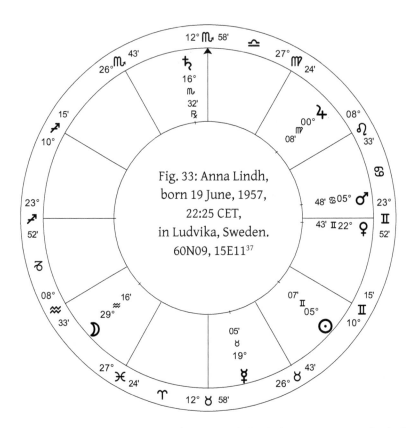

Fig. 33: Anna Lindh, born 19 June, 1957, 22:25 CET, in Ludvika, Sweden. 60N09, 15E11[37]

The nativity is a nocturnal one, with both luminaries too far below the horizon to qualify as hyleg. Of the remaining planets, Saturn occupies the strongest hylegiacal place, the midheaven. Does it have the dignities required to make it hyleg according to Ptolemy? It does: the Moon, luminary of the nocturnal sect, is in the terms, domicile and triplicity of Saturn; and Saturn in Scorpio also aspects the Moon in Aquarius by a whole-sign square. Ptolemy does not mention the need for a hyleg to be aspected by its own rulers as other authors do, but Saturn does receive such aspects, both from Mercury (ruler by terms) and from Mars (ruler by domicile and triplicity). Saturn is thus well-qualified to become hyleg in Anna Lindh's chart.

What of the anaereta? The obvious choice using Ptolemy's rules would be the other malefic, Mars, which is also consistent with death by stabbing. To find the likely time of death, we should then look for a direction between Mars or its aspects (particularly the square and opposition) and Saturn.

Using classical zodiacal aspects and proportional semi-arcs, the directions around the times of Lindh's Mars-Saturn contacts are as follows:[38]

Saturn square Mars converse	28°04′	
Saturn square Venus converse	32°23′	
[...]		
Saturn conjunct Mars converse	46°48′	(with latitude: 50°26′)
Saturn trine Jupiter direct	46°59′	
Saturn sextile Jupiter converse	47°55′	
Saturn conjunct Venus converse	51°51′	(with latitude: 53°21′)
Saturn opposition Mars direct	52°43′	(with latitude: 53°22′)

Once again, the 'converse' directions in this list are converse in the traditional sense of bringing the significator (Saturn, the hyleg) to the promissors rather than vice versa. All directions, direct and converse, are brought about by the natural primary motion from east to west.

Although all the directions between the hyleg and Mars are mixed with directions to the benefics, the combined impact of the converse conjunction with Mars and its direct opposition within the space of 6° proved fatal. Anna Lindh was stabbed in public on 10 September, 2003, and died from the resulting injuries on the following day, aged 46y 3m. Other pertinent directions around this time included the affliction of both the luminaries:

Sun square Mars converse	45°43′
Saturn opposition Moon direct with latitude	45°43′

It will be remembered that Ptolemy regards the affliction of the luminaries by the malefics as an indication of a violent and remarkable death. The Sun is also the ruler of the 8th house.

SUMMARY

❖ Predicting the length of life was one of the earliest uses of primary directions, and has retained its importance throughout their history. Such predictions were made by examining the directions of a single planet or point taken as the significator of life, most often referred to in later literature as the *hyleg*.

❖ Although classical sources give several variations of this technique, the method of Ptolemy has enjoyed the greatest esteem. Here, the hyleg is chosen according to detailed rules from among the Sun, Moon, ascendant, Part of Fortune, and the planets ruling them.

❖ Ptolemy allows two kinds of lethal directions: one where a malefic planet or its aspect is carried to the hyleg by the primary motion, and another where the hyleg itself, located in the western part of the sky, is brought down to the horizon. In the latter case, the arc of direction is modified by the conjunctions and aspects of other planets. These principles seem to be variations on older teachings. Both the time and the circumstances of death are supposedly determined by the directions.

❖ Other classical writers both before and after Ptolemy wanted the hyleg to be aspected by at least one of its planetary rulers, and attached great importance to this planet in determining the length of life. In medieval times it was even more emphasized, becoming known as the *alcochoden*.

❖ Medieval writers on the hyleg and alcochoden mixed Ptolemaic and pre-Ptolemaic principles with innovations of their own into an increasingly complex variety of methods. With the Renaissance, a general trend of 'return to Ptolemy' began, leading to the neo-Ptolemaic system pioneered by Placidus in the late 17th century and continued in Britain for some 200 years.

REFERENCES

1. Robbins 1940:271.
2. As Arabic is commonly written without vowels, the word has been vocalized both as *hīlāj* and *haylāj*; but as noted by Kunitzsch 1977:49 f, *hīlāj* is closer to the original Middle Persian word, and the medieval transcriptions all reflect a pronunciation with *ī* rather than *ay*. The same is true of the late Sanskrit borrowing *hillāja*, found in several texts of the *tājika* ('Persian') school of astrology present in India.
3. Certain older authors, being unfamiliar with other classical languages than Latin, Greek and Hebrew, mistakenly imagined the word *hyleg* to be derived from Hebrew *hālakh* 'go'; cf. Partridge 1693:137, Sibly 1826:463.
4. Pingree 1978:99, 329 f considers Chapter 35 of the 3rd century Sanskrit text *Yavanajātaka* an abortive attempt to introduce the concept of the 'prorogator' or hyleg in India; but in my opinion, the few verses constituting this chapter are too garbled for such a supposition to be more than guesswork.
5. Robbins 1940:270–307, 426–437.
6. The consideration of sect is a simple yet powerful key to prediction. I warmly recommend Robert Hand's booklet on the subject (Hand 1995b).
7. Some commentators on Ptolemy recommend taking the position of that luminary which, at the time of the opposition, happens to be above the horizon; but in my view, Ptolemy's use of the word *panselēnos* (πανσέληνος) 'Full Moon' for the opposition makes it unlikely that he intended the position of the Sun to be taken. Kolev 2008:21 ff similarly makes a case for using that point which *later*, at the time of birth, would be above the horizon, basing his argument on a disputed reading of a different passage of the *Tetrabiblos* (3.2, dealing with rectification of the ascendant by the method later known as *animodar*; see Robbins 1940:230 ff). Even if the reading is correct, it is by no means certain that Ptolemy meant for the procedure used in this context to be transferred to the determination of the hyleg.
8. Ptolemy's actual phrasing is unclear, but this seems the only meaningful interpretation. The text reads (Robbins 1940:278): εἰ δὲ καὶ ἀμφότερα τὰ φῶτα ἢ καὶ ὁ τῆς οἰκείας αἱρέσεως οἰκοδεσπότης ἐν τοῖς ἀφετικοῖς εἶεν τόποις, τὸν ἐν τῷ κυριωτέρῳ τόπῳ τῶν φωτῶν παραληπτέον, literally: 'And if both the luminaries, *or else* the ruler of the proper sect,

should be in the hylegiacal places, one should prefer the one of the luminaries [found] in the more powerful place' (emphasis mine). Taken literally, this instruction makes no sense: if both luminaries are *not* in hylegiacal places, but the ruler of the sect is, why should the luminaries be preferred? And if they should, why bring the ruler of the sect into the discussion at all? Most likely the intention of Ptolemy was simply to say that if *two potential hylegs* are in acceptable places, we should prefer the one in the stronger place. Hübner 1998:208 also notes that one manuscript has ἀφετικῶν 'of the hylegiacals' instead of φώτων (*sic*) 'of the luminaries'.

9. Signs 'beholding' each other are those rising in the same amount of time (in the tropical zodiac used by Ptolemy), as they are equidistant from the equinoctial and solstitial points; cf. the discussion of *antiscia* in Chapter 8. Signs of long ascension rise in more than 2 hours; signs of short ascension, in less. In Ptolemy's zodiac, the former are the six signs from Cancer to Sagittarius; the latter, those from Capricorn to Gemini.

10. These distances may not be orbs of aspect in the later sense, but rather related symbolically to the years assigned to the planets as their periods, Jupiter having 12 years and Venus 8; cf. Robbins 1940:442 ff.

11. The Project Hindsight translation of *Tetrabiblos* (Schmidt 1995:38) quotes a single illustration of these calculations taken from Hephaestio – regrettably, an erroneous one. This is immediately followed by a critical scholium by Leon the Philosopher denouncing the faulty example, but without any comment by the translator. The reader may thus be left in some doubt as to which of the older authors is correct; the answer is Leon.

12. Pingree 1986:128 f. The text is available in English translation as Schmidt 1994 and in German as Knobloch & Schönberger 2004, both translations unfortunately made somewhat inaccessible by idiosyncratic renderings of technical terms.

13. The doctrine of the hyleg requiring an aspect from one of its rulers is known to go back at least to the 1st century CE, as Hephaestio of Thebes quotes one line from Dorotheus' original *Pentateuch* (only fragments of which remain) verbatim on the subject; see Pingree 1976:369 f. According to Hephaestio, Dorotheus preferred the rulers of the terms, domicile, exaltation or triplicity, in that order.

14. For the years assigned to the planets, found also in other classical authors, as well as the Egyptian terms, see Appendix III.
15. Pingree 1986:131, also translated in Schmidt 1994:40 f; Knobloch & Schönberger 2004:130 f.
16. In accordance with astronomical convention, Neugebauer & Van Hoesen 1959:76 ff refer to the year 72 BCE as -71.
17. A preserved synopsis of Balbillus' lost work *Astrologumena* (CCAG 8.3:103 f) states: 'And he names four *hylegs* (ἀφέτας): Saturn, Mars, Sun, Moon.' This, however, is most probably a corrupt reading, as the Byzantine fragment containing the two Balbillus horoscopes states: 'And he says that there are four *destroyers* (ἀναιρέτας): Sun, Moon, Saturn, Mars.' It seems very unlikely that Balbillus should have regarded the same four planets, including the two natural malefics, as both givers and destroyers of life. The latter view is the common one, and agrees with both Vettius Valens ('And the destroyers are Saturn, Mars, Sun and Moon, while she is brought towards heliacal rising (φάσιν)', Pingree 1986:131) and Ptolemy ('the places of the maleficent planets, Saturn and Mars, destroy [...] When the moon is the prorogator [hyleg], the place of the sun also destroys', Robbins 1940:282 f).
18. Neugebauer & Van Hoesen 1959:77 translate: '[...] he computed the distance from Aries to Mars, and so long, he said, would be the length of life.' As Aries itself is not a point, such a statement carries no obvious meaning, and the translators think themselves 'probably entitled to interpret this procedure more accurately as measuring the arc between Mars (♏ 14) and the quartile [i.e., square] of the starter [i.e., hyleg], i.e. ♈ 4 [...] The result would be an arc of 50°' (additions in square brackets mine). There are at least two problems with this assumption: first, the aspect of the hyleg would then be carried towards the anaereta, rather than that of the anaereta towards the hyleg as is the normal procedure (used by Balbillus himself in his second preserved example); second, the arc in question would be 50° only of *zodiacal longitude*, which is not a mode of calculation used by other authors – certainly not by Vettius Valens, whose 'many similar discussions of the duration of life' are invoked by the translators. Calculated according to Vettius' preferred system of rising times, the arc in question would be some 35°; by proportional semi-arcs, some 45° – 47° depending on the precise time of birth. There is no evidence to suggest that Balbillus used zodiacal degrees. In the

place of such spurious methodological assumptions, I have accepted the critical editor's very reasonable suggestion that *Kriou* (Κριοῦ) 'Aries' is a copyist's error for *Kronou* (Κρόνου) 'Saturn' (CCAG 8.4:237). It may be noted that the implausible suggestions of Neugebauer & Van Hoesen are accepted uncritically by Beck 2007:121 ff.

19. Again according to Hephaestio, writing in the early 5th century (Pingree 1976:369 f), Dorotheus used the Sun, Moon, Part of Fortune, prenatal syzygy and ascendant as potential hylegs, but viewed only the 1st, 10th and 11th houses as hylegiacal places.

20. 'Umar and other medieval writers include the Moon and ascendant as mutual anaeretas, as they are considered to be of opposite natures; cf. Hand 1997:17. Vettius Valens, as seen in note 17 above, includes the Moon as anaereta until its heliacal rising – misleadingly translated by Knobloch & Schönberger 2004:131 as: '[...] der Mond, *wenn* er in Erscheinung tritt' (emphasis mine). Vettius and many other classical and medieval authors also include the terms of the malefics among the anaeretas.

21. Decan or face is an equal division of each sign into three parts, for which various rulership schemes exist.

22. The Arabic word (with variants such as *al-kadhudāh, al-kadhudāh;* Dykes 2008 consistently uses *kadukhudhāh*) is thus not a corrupt transcription of *oikodespotēs* itself, as supposed by Bouché-Leclercq 1899:411, but of a Persian translation of the same word. The Latin variants are many, ranging from *alcocoden* to strange mutations such as *atelchodela* or *acolhodebia;* see Kunitzsch 1977:35 f.

23. Holden 2002:16 f.

24. Holden 2008b:57.

25. Holden 2008b:60.

26. Loc. cit.

27. Cooper [1814] 2004:164. The full discussion of Gustav II Adolf's nativity is found on pp. 163–169. The addition in square brackets is mine.

28. As discussed in Chapter 8, the crepuscular arcs of Placidus did not find much support even among his followers. Partridge 1697:126 ff proposes yet another birth time for Gustav II Adolf, giving an ascendant of some 8° of Sagittarius, and directs Saturn's parallel of declination to the Sun by proportional semi-arcs at the age of 37y 10m, followed by the

opposition of Saturn and square of Mars.

29. Worsdale 1828:272.
30. Worsdale 1828:290.
31. Worsdale 1828:297.
32. Worsdale 1828:90. The full discussion of the nativity is found on pp. 90–99.
33. Worsdale 1828:91.
34. See Cooper 2004:79. The hyleg will then have reached its mundane semi-square to the ascendant. Placidus, whose theory of aspects was based on music, here gives as his reason that 'in the semi-quadrate's distance, sounds begin to arrive at a degree of harmony'.
35. Worsdale 1828:97.
36. Worsdale 1828:98. Worsdale is referring not to the traditional system of terms or bounds, but to his own (insufficiently explained) innovation; cf. Chapter 2. Additions in square brackets are mine.
37. Municipal registers erroneously list Lindh's place of birth as Enskede, her parents' place of residence at the time. She was in fact born in Ludvika, near her paternal grandparents' residence in nearby Snöån, where her parents were visiting (see article in *Dala-Demokraten*, 14 May, 2004).
38. Directions including latitude have been given only for the conjunction and opposition, as there is no consensus on how to assign latitude to the remaining aspects.

10

Primary Directions and Other
Predictive Techniques

As discussed in Chapter 6, primary directions were traditionally used to identify the expected year of an event or series of events, but not the precise date or even month. Over the centuries, astrologers have employed a number of other predictive techniques to identify more closely the times at which a particular direction will take effect. This chapter offers an overview of the most commonly used techniques.

Profections

Like primary directions, profections have been in use since classical antiquity. In modern terminology, they are a form of *symbolic directions*; in other words, they are not based upon any actual motion found in nature. For this reason some astrological reformers, like Morin and Placidus, rejected them out of hand. To Ptolemy, however, profections were the first technique to be considered after directions:

> We shall discover the general chronocrators [rulers of time], then, in the manner described [i.e., by primary directions], and the annual chronocrators by setting out from each of the prorogatory places [i.e., the significators], in the order of the signs, the number of years from birth, one year to each sign, and taking the ruler of the last sign.[1]

Ptolemy describes both monthly and daily profections, but most relevant are the *annual* profections, by which the ascendant or some other significator in the radix is moved 30° forward along the zodiac for every year of life (and therefore returns to its original position every 12 years). In the form discussed here, this is a continuous movement, where a month corresponds to approximately 2°30', and a day to 5'. William Lilly writes:

> We make use of Annuall Profections to distinguish and know particular times, *viz.* the Moneths and Dayes of that Yeer, in which a successfull or

unhappy Direction doth fall: For when it is required at what time, or what Moneth, or neer unto what day the Event of a Direction shall appear; we then repair to our Profectionall figures. Considering what manner of Direction is then in force, and whether it be good or bad; Who is the *Significator*, who the *Promittor*; for *Profections* of themselves without Directions are not of much validity, or effect little; so also Directions are lesse powerfull and valid, when they are contradicted by *Profections* and *Transits* of a contrary influence.[2]

Lilly goes on to state that the profections involving the significator and promissor in a current direction should be particularly examined, and that the effects of the direction may be delayed until a profection of similar nature is formed.

To illustrate the method, let us return to the chart discussed in Chapter 5, where the midheaven is partilely squared by Mars (fig. 34). When this

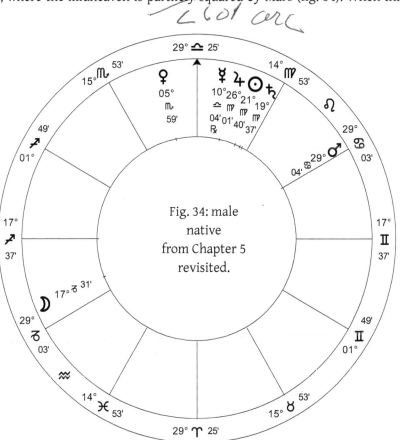

Fig. 34: male native from Chapter 5 revisited.

Fig. 35: Jupiter's profection to the
square of radical Mars at 25y 1m.

square was directed to Jupiter, ruler of the ascendant, the native suffered a professional setback. As Jupiter was later directed to the square of Venus, ruler of the 10th in the 10th, the situation was remedied after some effort.

The first direction (Mars square Jupiter) had an arc of 24°46′ but took effect at the age of 25y 1m. At this time the native's job application was disqualified. Jupiter's profected position was then partilely square Mars on the midheaven (fig. 35).

The second direction (Venus square Jupiter) had an arc of 25°20′ but took effect at the age of 25y 8m, at which time the native was accepted for an academic post. By profection, Venus was then in the 1st house closely square Jupiter (fig. 36).

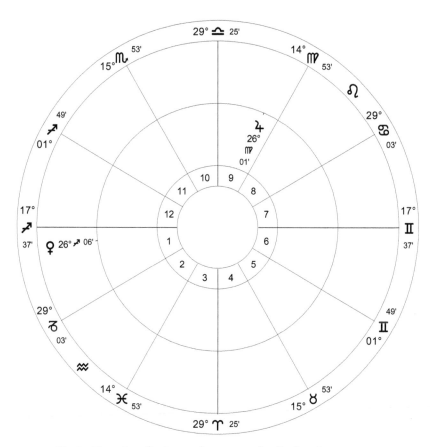

Fig. 36: Venus' profection to the square of radical Jupiter at 25y 8m.

While results are not always so neat, it has been my experience that profections are generally quite reliable as triggers of primary directions. As a variant example, we may take the chart of Joseph Ratzinger (Pope Benedict XVI) discussed in Chapter 6.

Ratzinger was elected pope, as we have seen, at the direction of Jupiter's trine to the Sun with an arc of 76°43', corresponding to 77y 10m by the key of Naibod. The event actually took place at 78y 0m, at which time all points in the chart were 180° removed from their radical positions. Thus, while there was no profectional aspect between significator and promissor, both these planets partilely aspected their *own* respective natal positions, the Sun also ruling the profected ascendant.

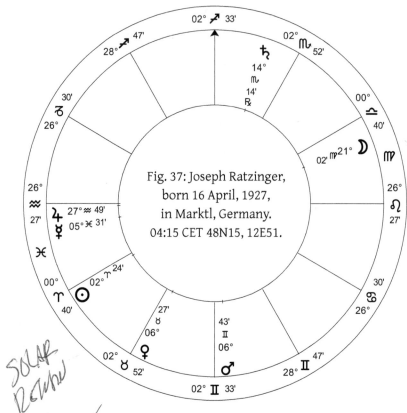

Fig. 37: Joseph Ratzinger,
born 16 April, 1927,
in Marktl, Germany.
04:15 CET 48N15, 12E51.

Revolutions

A technique which has often been combined with annual profections is that of revolutions or, as they are known in modern astrology, solar returns. These are charts cast for the time of the Sun's return to its exact zodiacal position in the radix. This time will differ depending on whether the tropical or sidereal zodiac is used, unless the tropical revolution is corrected for precession (as advocated by some modern tropical astrologers). Opinion is also divided on whether revolution charts should be cast for the place of birth or for the place at which the native finds himself at the time of the revolution.

The latter view was espoused by Morin, who, having rejected profections, made revolutions the second most important part of his predictive system and devoted one whole book of his *Astrologia Gallica* to them. To Morin, revolutions held a middle position between the radix and its directions on one hand and transits on the other:

[The virtue of a direction] cannot be reduced at that time from potentiality to action except by something actual: namely, a revolution conformable to the future event, and conformable transits of the planets by body or by aspect through suitable places in the geniture, which are first of all the places of the significator and the promittor, or places related in signification to them. And yet conformable revolutions and conformable transits do not always occur at that precise time, or if there is a conformable revolution for the year, there will not be a conformable transit for the day corresponding to the arc of direction, but either both, or the second, and especially a suitable transit will come before the precise time or after it.[3]

Morin also frequently included the revolutions of the Moon in his judgments, in order to determine the likely month of an expected event. Despite the faith which he put in the method, however, his lunar revolutions were often miscalculated (largely due to imperfect tables), sometimes so much as to invalidate much of his reasoning.[4]

Revolutions are far more complex than profections, with conflicting opinions on both calculation and interpretation. With so many variables to consider, it is difficult to evaluate the usefulness of the technique as an auxiliary to primary directions. In my own experience, irrespective of the method of calculation, I have not found revolutions as useful a tool as profections.

In retrospect, however, certain revolutions do stand out, one instance being that of Joseph Ratzinger's 78th revolution (occurring three days prior to the papal election). Whether erected for his birth place or for his residence at the Vatican, the angles and other house cusps of the sidereal (or precessed) revolution closely repeat their radical degrees. The ascendant of the revolution was therefore conjunct radical Jupiter, while the exalted Sun again trined the midheaven, which was also conjunct the Part of Fortune.

Secondary directions and progressions

One astrologer who did not share Morin's views on the importance of revolutions was Placidus, who wrote:

The revolution, as taught by some, I have not seen, though in reality they may possess some virtue, but only according to the constitution of the stars [i.e., planets] to the places of the prorogators [i.e., significators] of the nativity, and their places of direction, but no farther [...] therefore, let any one, if he pleases, observe the return of the years, but at the same time, let him not place so great a value on them, as some authors usually do; who, from the constitution of the stars, judge of the Sun's return in the same manner as of the nativity; so that they are not afraid to dissent from the same, nor even from the directions.[5]

Having rejected both profections and, for all practical purposes, revolutions, Placidus was in need of another auxiliary technique. As discussed in Chapter 2, he found it in his secondary directions, familiar to most present-day astrologers as *(secondary) progressions* and calculated by the simple formula 'a day for a year'. The technique as applied by its inventor, however, was rather different from what is generally practised today. Placidus was clear that the secondary directions were a mere supplement to the primary, and concerned only those Ptolemaic significators which possessed secondary motion – that is to say, the Sun and Moon:

> [W]e must observe, when the luminaries are posited in any aspect of the stars [i.e., planets]; for if with the fortunes, they conduce to happiness and good health; if with the unfortunate, and from an hostile ray or parallel of declination, they portend misery and distress in those years which depend on those days these aspects happen on.[6]

Only in relatively rare cases could another planet be admitted to the dignity of hyleg or significator of life, and its secondary directions examined.

Placidus also invented another technique, which he called *progressions*, based on the equation 'a synodic month for a year'. Requiring slightly more calculation than secondary directions, these progressions seem to have disappeared during the great simplification process of the late 19th and early 20th centuries, although a similar technique was invented some fifty years later by German astrologer E. H. Troinski, who called it *tertiary directions*.

I have no experience of Placidean progressions, and have not generally found secondary directions helpful in determining the time of a primary direction, although admittedly I limit myself – unlike Placidus, but like Ptolemy – to the conjunction and four classical aspects.[7]

Transits and ingresses

For most modern astrologers, the first auxiliary technique to spring to mind is perhaps transits. These are not anywhere as prominent in classical texts as they are in current practice, although Ptolemy does give importance to the transits of the planets through the 'places' – probably referring to entire signs – of the significators: Saturn transits to the natal significators; Jupiter transits to the places of the annual profection; Moon transits to those of the daily profection; and the transits of the remaining planets to those of the monthly profections.[8]

Both Renaissance and modern authors have given transits a role in triggering primary directions. To Morin they were the final link in a chain of prediction, and should be viewed not only in the light of the radix chart and its directions, but also of the solar and lunar revolutions – a daunting task, as Morin himself realized, although he argued that the methods of 'the old or common Astrology' were equally demanding if seen in their entirety.[9]

Morin taught that directions are actualized by 'conformable' transits – that is, transits indicating the same sort of events as the directions, though not necessarily involving the same planets. Most powerful, however, are the transits of the significator and promissor themselves (or of their rulers, when either significator or promissor is a mere point) over their own or each other's radical places, and particularly when they are also conjunct or in appropriate aspect with each other in transit.

To the transits of planets over the radical places of significator and promissor, Placidus added the *ingresses*, or transits to the *directional places* of the same points.[10] The use of ingresses was particularly advocated in the 20th century by E. C. Kühr, who claimed a very high degree of accuracy for them, often indicating the very day or even hour (!) of an event. Kühr wrote:

> Much has already been written on the important topic of the triggering of directions. Morin regarded transits as the primary triggers, and every practitioner is sure to know of many cases to be put forward in confirmation of his opinion. But in at least as many, if not in more numerous cases, triggering transits are sought in vain. There must be a reason for this failure. It is to be found in the fact that Morin examined only transits to the *radical* places, when in fact one should examine transits to the *directional* places! For *it is the directional places, not the radical, which are active at the time of a direction!*[11]

Although primary directions are not based on the motion of planets through the zodiac (secondary motion), the zodiacal degrees being carried by the primary motion across the location held by a planet or point at birth can be viewed as a progress of that point through the signs. The ascendant and midheaven are the most obvious examples: although the circles of the horizon and meridian are in fact fixed in relation to the place of observation, the constant rising and culmination of the zodiacal signs may be – and often is – described as the progression of the ascendant and midheaven through the zodiac. In exactly the same manner, any planet or other chart point may be regarded as fixed in its natal position, and a zodiac degree reaching that position in the sky becomes the 'directional place' of the planet.

The directional place of the *fixed* element in a primary direction needs no calculation, as it is identical with the radical place of the moving element. If, for instance, the sextile of the Sun is located at 28° Aquarius in the radix and is directed to the ascendant, 28° Aquarius then becomes the directional place of the ascendant. If the same sextile is directed to Jupiter, 28° Aquarius becomes the directional place of Jupiter. In fact, Kühr argues, when a transit over a radical place does seem to trigger a direction, this is because that part of the zodiac is simultaneously the directional place of the other element in the direction.

But Kühr also recommends using ingresses to the *moving* element in a direction. Calculating the directional place of this element without recourse to tables involves the same difficulty present in the calculation of Placidean house cusps, as we ask the question: 'Which part of the zodiac will, at a given time, have reached proportional point X in its semi-arc?' The answer can only be reached by a time-consuming process of successive approximations and corrections.

Kühr's preferred system of directions was not strictly speaking the Ptolemaic or Placidean semi-arc system, but rather Placidean directions 'under the pole' (see Chapter 8), and he calculated the directional places used for ingresses by the same method. He also differed from Placidus in using the Naibod key (see Chapter 6), defined 'converse directions' in the modern way as directions *against* the primary motion and employed the transsaturnian planets Uranus and Neptune. The two latter factors more than doubled the number of potential hit points for his ingresses.

As the zodiac keeps passing over the fixed points of the natal chart by the primary motion after birth, at any given time each of these points will have a directional place in the zodiac; and this place my be transited by planets whether there currently is a primary direction involving the point in question or not. If the transiting planet were angular or otherwise strongly placed in the natal chart, Kühr considered such an independent ingress as powerful enough in itself to indicate an event – particularly if the planet were a slow-moving one and transited the directional place by conjunction or opposition. Kühr referred to such transits as 'small directions'.

While I have seen a number of instances of relevant transits over directional points, I would not go so far as to assert that they are always present. At the time of Joseph Ratzinger's election to the papacy, Saturn, ruler of the ascendant, was transiting the degree of Jupiter's trine – in other words, the directional degree of the Sun.

Diurnal and hourly directions

Some astrological authors have devised methods of calculating separate sets of faster-moving primary directions, either from the natal chart itself or from the revolution, as an aid to more precise timing. The entire circle of 360° is then made to correspond to (approximately) one year, so that one day covers just under 1° of directional motion. Kühr argued that the technique as applied to the radix is inherent in the use of the Naibod key:

> In the space of a mean solar day, however, the duration of which we equate with a year of life in directions, all places move 360° + 59′ 8.33″ [...] Thus, *in primary directions* the daily rotation of the circle = 360° is not considered, but only the constant daily increment of 59′ 8.33″ is employed as the directional motion [...] But on the other hand, the total motion of 360° 59′ 8.33″ in a day – that is, in a directional year – should be accepted as a *second* key for a class of *sub*-directions which we will label *diurnal directions*.[12]

The diurnal arc of direction for any date is therefore found by multiplying the number of days passed since the native's latest birthday by 0°59′08.33″ and adding the resulting arc to its 'normal' arc of primary direction (with the Naibod key) for the same date. Kühr applied this arc to points already involved in a direction, looking for repeated contacts between significator and promissor. In doing so, he indiscriminately mixed directions with and against the primary motion, thus doubling the number of possible hits. My own experiences with these diurnal directions have been very limited, and not encouraging.

Similar directions have been applied to the annual (solar) revolution at least since medieval times. In the 10th century, al-Qabīsī, relying on older sources, wrote towards the end of his account of primary directions or *tasyīr*:

> If this is the ascendant of the transfer of the year [i.e., revolution], whether it is for the world or for nativities, then the *tasyīr* of its indicators [i.e., significators] is according to the *tasyīr* of one day for every degree. Some of them consider that the *tasyīr* of the indicators of the year is one day for every 59 minutes and eight seconds.[13]

Seven centuries later, Morin made use not only of the solar, but even of the lunar revolutions, in the latter case equating 360° of direction with the time required for the Moon to complete one circle of the zodiac – approximately 1h 49m of clock-time per degree. Although Morin did not direct against the primary motion like Kühr, he viewed the radix, solar revolution and lunar revolution in a cumulative fashion, so that chart elements from a higher level could be 'projected' onto a lower. In a solar revolution, therefore, all planets and house cusps exist in two versions (those of the revolution itself and those imported from the natal chart); and in a lunar revolution, in three versions (lunar, solar, and natal)! It would be rather surprising *not* to find 'relevant' directions after the fact with this method; and correspondingly difficult to use it for actual prognostication. I have not experimented with it.[14]

SUMMARY

❖ Astrologers have traditionally employed several techniques to identify the times at which a primary direction will take effect. Of particular importance are the annual profections, based on a wholly symbolic motion of 30° per year. Profections involving the significator and promissor of a current direction are especially relevant.

❖ Another common auxiliary technique is that of revolutions or solar returns, strongly advocated by Morin, who rejected profections. The many possible variations involved in casting and interpreting revolutions make this technique difficult to evaluate.

❖ Placidus rejected both profections and revolutions in favour of so-called secondary directions and progressions, based on secondary motion through the zodiac. These were not intended as independent techniques, but as supplements to primary directions, and concerned only aspects formed to the Sun and Moon.

❖ Transits did not play a prominent part in ancient and medieval astrology, but were used by both Morin and Placidus as the final link in a chain of prediction. Transits to the directional places of relevant points were termed *ingresses* by Placidus. In the 20th century, E. C. Kühr claimed that only ingresses, and not transits to radical places, were relevant in triggering primary directions, and could even indicate events not shown by directions.

❖ Separate sets of fast-moving primary directions based on the solar revolution were calculated by some medieval astrologers. Morin calculated directions from both solar and lunar revolutions to find the precise time of events; and Kühr devised a similar method of 'diurnal directions' based on the natal chart itself.

REFERENCES

1. Robbins 1940:453. Additions in square brackets are mine.
2. Lilly 1659:718 f.
3. Holden 1994:89; additions in square brackets mine.
4. Examples may be found in many places throughout Holden 2002.
5. Cooper [1814] 2004:127 f; additions in square brackets mine. Morin took great exception to this statement: 'I give warning that [the reader] should take note and then be convinced of how false and erroneous is that new doctrine of Didacus Prittus Pelusiensis [... who] has rejected both the annual and monthly revolutions, which he takes absolutely no account of in his judgments. He promises [to publish] demonstrations of his doctrine, which are expected [by us] to be, not demonstrations of truth (as I easily deduce from his *Theses*), but [rather] as demonstrations of his own hallucinations' (Holden 2002:117).
6. Cooper [1814] 2004:110; additions in square brackets mine.
7. Some astrological authors have pointed out, after the fact, that by secondary direction the Sun was conjunct the ascendant and trine the midheaven in Joseph Ratzinger's chart at the time that he was elected Pope. This is quite true; but the same configuration had been in effect for three decades before the event.
8. See Robbins 1940:453 ff.
9. See Holden 2004: 78 ff.
10. See Cooper [1814] 2004:26 f, 109 ff.
11. Kühr 1936:257. My summary of Kühr's use of ingresses below is based on pp. 245–263 of the same work.
12. Kühr 1936:264. As the Sun moves an average of 0°59′08″ (measured either in longitude or in right ascension) per day, the mean solar day is slightly longer than a sidereal day.
13. Burnett et al. 2004:127.
14. Morin's own description and examples of the method are found in Holden 2002:108 ff, and also discussed in Kühr 1936:285 ff.

Appendix I

Formulae for Calculating Primary Directions

With a little patience, primary directions can be calculated by hand using an inexpensive scientific calculator with sexagesimal notation and trigonometrical functions. In order to calculate the primary directions of any planet in a chart, we need to know:

- the right ascension (RA) and declination (δ) of the planet;
- the geographical latitude of the birth place (Φ);
- the right ascension of the midheaven (RAMC).

The RAMC is the Local Sidereal Time expressed in degrees, each hour of LST equalling 15°. To illustrate the procedures, we shall use the chart from p. 54, and the following values:

- RAMC = 337°58′ (LST = 22:31:52)
- Φ of birth place = +58°16′

Definitions of technical terms and concepts are found in Chapter 3 and in the Glossary.

It is advisable to go through the steps below in order. However, it should be noted that steps 4a, 4b and 4c represent three different methods of directing one non-angular planet or point to another.

1a. Finding the declination and right ascension of a planet or point *in zodiaco*

If a planet's right ascension and declination are unknown, they can be derived from the planet's tropical longitude (λ) and, optionally, latitude (β), along with the obliquity of the ecliptic (ε), which is currently around 23.44°. In our example chart, Mercury has a tropical longitude of 128°25′ and a latitude of +0°12′.

Formulae which include latitude are used when directing the actual bodies of the planets (*in mundo*), rather than their zodiacal or ecliptical positions (*in zodiaco*). The values of planetary δ and RA given by astrological software are usually *in mundo*.

The values of δ and RA *in zodiaco* are those of a given point on the ecliptic, with 0° latitude. To find them we need only the tropical longitude of the planet or point and the obliquity of the ecliptic. For the Sun, which by definition is always on the ecliptic, we use only these simpler formulae. We begin by finding the δ:

$$\delta = \sin^{-1}(\sin \varepsilon \times \sin \lambda)$$
$$= \sin^{-1}(\sin 23.44 \times \sin 128°25')$$
$$= \sin^{-1}(0.39779 \times 0.78351)$$
$$= 18°10'$$

If the result is a negative value, the planet or zodiacal point has southern declination.

To find the RA of any point on the ecliptic, we must first determine its equatorial distance from the nearest equinoctial point, where the equator and ecliptic intersect (0° Aries and 0° Libra in the tropical zodiac). We shall call this the *equinoctial distance* (ED):

$$ED = \tan^{-1}(\cos \varepsilon \times \tan \lambda)$$
$$= \tan^{-1}(\cos 23.44° \times \tan 128°25')$$
$$= \tan^{-1}(0.91748 \times -1.26093)$$
$$= -49°10'$$

We then transform this position into RA, reckoned forwards from the vernal equinoctial point (0° tropical Aries), as follows:

$$RA = ED \text{ if } \lambda < 90°$$
$$RA = 180° + ED \text{ if } 90° < \lambda < 270°$$
$$RA = 360° + ED \text{ if } 270° < \lambda$$
$$= 180° + -49°10'$$
$$= 130°50'$$

Note that when the ED is a negative value, adding it equals subtracting the corresponding positive value.

1b. Finding the declination and right ascension of a planet *in mundo*
For directions *in mundo* we use the δ and RA of the actual bodies of the planets. To calculate these we need formulae which include latitude (β). We begin as before with δ:

$$\delta = \sin^{-1}(\sin \varepsilon \times \sin \lambda \times \cos \beta + \cos \varepsilon \times \sin \beta)$$
$$= \sin^{-1}(\sin 23.44 \times \sin 128°25' \times \cos 0°12' + \cos 23.44 \times \sin 0°12')$$
$$= \sin^{-1}(0.39779 \times 0.78351 \times 0.99999 + 0.91748 \times 0.00349)$$
$$= 18°21'$$

Using this value, we then determine the ED:

$$ED = \cos^{-1}(\cos \lambda \times \cos \beta / \cos \delta)$$
$$= \cos^{-1}(\cos 128°25' \times \cos 0°12' / \cos 18°21')$$
$$= \cos^{-1}(-0.62138 \times 0.99999 / 0.94915)$$
$$= 130°54'$$

Finally, we transform ED into RA:

$$RA = ED \text{ if } \lambda < 180°$$
$$RA = 360° - ED \text{ if } 180° < \lambda$$
$$= 130°54'$$

This procedure is reliable except when λ is very close to 0° or 180°, in which case the actual body of the planet may be on the opposite side of the equator. The correctness of the RA may be verified with the following formula, allowing a very small margin (less than 1″) for rounding errors:

$$\sin RA \times \cos \delta = \cos \varepsilon \times \sin \lambda \times \cos \beta - \sin \varepsilon \times \sin \beta$$
$$\sin 130°54' \times \cos 18°21' =$$
$$= 0.75585 \times 0.94915$$
$$= 0°43'02.69''$$

$$\cos 23.44 \times \sin 128°25' \times \cos 0°12' - \sin 23.44 \times \sin 0°12' =$$
$$= 0.91748 \times 0.78351 \times 0.99999 - 0.39779 \times 0.00349$$
$$= 0°43'02.85''$$

If the two values do not match, subtracting the supposed RA from 360° will give the correct RA.

2. Directing a planet or point to the meridian (MC or IC)

This is the simplest form of direction, performed by a straightforward subtraction of right ascension. The right ascension of the lower midheaven, RAIC, is always opposite the RAMC.

$$RAIC = RAMC \pm 180°$$
$$= 337°58' - 180°$$
$$= 157°58'$$

The distance of the planet from either of these points is called its *right* or *meridian distance* (MD) – upper MD if to the upper midheaven (MC), lower MD if to the lower midheaven (IC). *If the 0° point on the equator (0° tropical Aries) should fall between the planet and the angle concerned, 360° must be added to the lower number.* We shall use the zodiacal position of Mercury:

upper MD   = RA planet - RAMC
$$= (360° + 130°50') - 337°58'$$
$$= 152°52'$$

lower MD   = RA planet - RAIC
$$= 130°50' - 157°58'$$
$$= -27°08'$$

If the result is a positive number, *the meridian distance is the arc of direction to the MC or IC*, as the case may be, in direct motion. If the result is a negative number, the meridian distance would be an arc of direction only 'conversely' in the modern sense (against the primary motion). In our example chart, Mercury's direct arc of direction to the MC is 152°52', and thus too great to be perfected during the native's lifetime.

3. Directing a planet or point to the horizon (ascendant or descendant)

This is accomplished by subtraction of oblique ascension (OA) or descension (OD). The oblique ascension of the ascendant is always 90° greater than the RAMC, while the oblique descension of the descendant is 90° less than the RAMC.

OA Asc	= RAMC + 90°
	= 337°58' + 90°
	= (427°58' - 360°) = 67°58'

OD Desc	= RAMC - 90°
	= 337°58' - 90°
	= 247°58'

For a planet located in the eastern half of the chart, the oblique ascension is found by adding the planet's *ascensional difference* (AD) to its right ascension; for a planet in the western half, the oblique descension is found by subtracting the AD from the RA. *This process is reversed for births in the southern hemisphere.* The AD depends on the planet's declination and the geographical latitude of birth:

AD	$= \sin^{-1} (\tan \delta \times \tan \Phi)$
	$= \sin^{-1} (\tan 18°10' \times \tan +58°16')$
	$= \sin^{-1} (0.32814 \times 1.61703)$
	$= 32°03'$

OA (eastern planet)	= RA - AD
OD (western planet)	= RA + AD
	= 130°50' - 32°03'
	= 98°47'

Once more, *if the 0° point on the equator (0° tropical Aries) should fall between the planet and the angle concerned, 360° must be added to the lower number.* Note that if the AD is a negative value, adding it to the RA equals subtracting the corresponding positive value, and vice versa. For births in the southern hemisphere, the - and + signs in the formulae for oblique ascension and descension should be reversed.

Having determined the OA/OD of both planet and ascendant/descendant, subtraction yields the horizontal distance (HD):

HD in the east	= OA planet - OA Asc
HD in the west	= OD planet - OD Desc
	= 98°47′ - 67°58′
	= 30°49′

If the result is positive, *the horizontal distance is the arc of direction* to the ascendant or descendant in direct motion. If it is negative, the horizontal distance could become an arc of direction only 'conversely' in the modern sense (against the primary motion). In the example chart, Mercury's direct arc of direction to the ascendant is 30°49′.

4a. Directing one planet or point to another by proportional semi-arcs
Within its own quadrant, a planet's meridian distance and horizontal distance together make up its semi-arc – diurnal (DSA) if the planet is above the horizon, nocturnal (NSA) if below it. Both meridian distance and horizontal distance must be treated as positive numbers (no minus signs).

DSA = HD + upper MD
NSA = HD + lower MD
= 30°49′ + 27°08′
= 57°57′

The difference between either semi-arc and 180° will give the other semi-arc:

DSA = 180° - NSA
= 180° - 57°57′
= 122°03′
NSA = 180° - DSA
= 180° - 122°03′
= 57°57′

In directing one planet or point to another by the semi-arc method, we begin by determining the proportional distance reached by the fixed point (FixP) in its semi-arc, as measured from the meridian. For a point above the horizon, we use the relation between its diurnal semi-arc and upper meridian distance; for a point below the horizon, as in our example, we use the nocturnal semi-arc and lower meridian distance.

proportional distance FixP	= MD FixP / SA FixP
	= 27°08′ / 57°57′
	= 0.46822

We then find the corresponding distance *in the corresponding semi-arc* for the moving point (MovP). Let the zodiacal position of Mars be the point directed to that of Mercury. Mars has a nocturnal semi-arc of 60°32′.

projected MD MovP	= proportional distance FixP × SA MovP
	= 0.46822 × 60°32′
	= 28°21′

Finally, we find the difference between this projected distance of the moving point from the meridian and its natal distance from the same meridian, which will yield the arc of direction. The lower meridian distance of Mars in the example chart is 22°31′.

arc of direction	= natal MD - projected MD
	= 28°21′ - 22°31′
	= 5°50′

Thus, the arc of direction for Mars conjunct Mercury *in zodiaco* by proportional semi-arcs is 5°50′, or 5.83°. The corresponding direction *in mundo* is found by using the mundane values of RA and δ for the planets involved.

4b. Directing one planet or point to another by Placidean circles of position ('under the pole')
This method uses the proportional semi-arc of the fixed planet or point to create an artificial horizon (circle of position) to which the moving planet

or point is then directed. The first step is to calculate the ascensional difference (AD) of the fixed point at this new 'horizon', known as its AD *under its own pole* (φ).

$$
\begin{aligned}
\text{AD under } \varphi \;&= \text{MD} / \text{SA} \times \text{AD} \\
&= 27°08' / 57°57' \times 32°03' \\
&= 15°00'
\end{aligned}
$$

It is important to include the positive or negative value of the AD. From the result we then extract the value of φ itself, that is, the geographical latitude to which the new 'horizon' corresponds (known as the *elevation of the pole*):

$$
\begin{aligned}
\varphi \;&= \tan^{-1}(\sin \text{AD under } \varphi / \tan \delta) \\
&= \tan^{-1}(\sin 15°00' / \tan 18°10') \\
&= \tan^{-1}(0.25882 / 0.32814) \\
&= 38°16'
\end{aligned}
$$

Next, we find the difference between the RA of the fixed point and its ascensional difference under φ. If the fixed point is located in the eastern half of the chart, we subtract from the RA to find the *oblique ascension (OA) under φ*; if the point is in the western half, we add to the RA to find the *oblique descension (OD) under φ*.

$$
\begin{aligned}
\text{OA eastern planet under } \varphi \;&= \text{RA} - \text{AD under } \varphi \\
\text{OD western planet under } \varphi \;&= \text{RA} + \text{AD under } \varphi \\
&= 130°50' - 15°00' \\
&= 115°50'
\end{aligned}
$$

As before, the + and - signs must be reversed for births in the southern hemisphere.

Our next step is to find the ascensional difference of the second element of the direction – the moving planet or point – relative to the same artificial horizon, that is, under the same φ. Mars has a δ of +16°55' and RA of 135°27'.

AD of MovP under φ of FixP $= \sin^{-1} (\tan \delta \text{ MovP} \times \tan \varphi \text{ FixP})$

$= \sin^{-1} (\tan 16°55' \times \tan 38°16')$

$= \sin^{-1} (0.30414 \times 0.78881)$

$= 13°53'$

Once again, we add this new ascensional difference to, or subtract it from, the RA of the point in question. Note that it is the eastern or western placement of the *fixed* point which determines whether we want the OA or OD.

OA of MovP under φ of eastern FixP   = RA of MovP - AD under φ of FixP

OD of MovP under φ of western FixP   = RA of MovP + AD under φ of FixP

$= 135°27' - 13°53'$

$= 121°34'$

It then remains only to subtract the new OA or OD of the fixed point from that of the moving point:

arc of direction   = OA/OD of MovP under φ of FixP - OA/OD of FixP under own φ

$= 121°34' - 115°50'$

$= 5°44'$

Thus, the arc of direction for Mars conjunct Mercury *in zodiaco* by Placidean circles of position is 5°44', or 5.73°. The corresponding direction *in mundo* is again found by using the mundane values of RA and δ for the planets involved. (Some astrologers have advocated a hybrid variety, where *in mundo* values are used for the fixed but not for the moving point.)

4c. Directing one planet or point to another by Regiomontanian circles of position

Regiomontanus directions are similarly based on artificial horizons passing through the fixed point, but in this case intersecting the north and south points of the natal horizon. To calculate these directions, we begin by determining three auxiliary angles, which we may call simply X, Y and Z:

$$
\begin{aligned}
X \quad &= \tan^{-1}(\tan \delta \text{ FixP} / \cos \text{ upper MD FixP}) \\
&= \tan^{-1}(\tan 18°10' / \cos 152°52') \\
&= \tan^{-1}(0.32814 / -0.88995) \\
&= -20°14'
\end{aligned}
$$

The MD is treated as a positive number (no minus sign).

$$
\begin{aligned}
Y \quad &= \Phi - X \\
&= 58°16' - (-20°14') \\
&= 78°30'
\end{aligned}
$$

Note again that subtracting a negative number equals adding the corresponding positive number.

$$
\begin{aligned}
Z \quad &= \tan^{-1}(\cos Y / (\tan \text{ MD FixP} \times \cos X)) \\
&= \tan^{-1}(\cos 78°30' / (\tan 152°52' \times \cos -20°14')) \\
&= \tan^{-1}(0.19937 / (-0.51246 \times 0.93829)) \\
&= -22°31'
\end{aligned}
$$

This last angle is used to determine the pole (φ) of the fixed point (note that this value is *not* identical with that of the Placidean pole in the previous method):

$$
\begin{aligned}
\varphi \quad &= \sin^{-1}(\sin \Phi \times \cos Z) \\
&= \sin^{-1}(\sin 58°16' \times \cos -22°31') \\
&= \sin^{-1}(0.85051 \times 0.92377) \\
&= 51°47'
\end{aligned}
$$

Using this value and the declination of the fixed point of the direction, we then calculate the ascensional difference of the fixed point under its own pole and its oblique ascension or descension as in the previous method (remembering to reverse the + and - signs for births in the southern hemisphere):

$$
\begin{aligned}
\text{AD under } \varphi &= \sin^{-1}(\tan \delta \times \tan \varphi) \\
&= \sin^{-1}(\tan 18°10' \times \tan 51°47') \\
&= \sin^{-1}(0.32814 \times 1.27001) \\
&= 24°38'
\end{aligned}
$$

$$
\begin{aligned}
\text{OA eastern planet under } \varphi &= \text{RA} - \text{AD under } \varphi \\
\text{OD western planet under } \varphi &= \text{RA} + \text{AD under } \varphi \\
&= 130°50' - 24°38' \\
&= 106°12'
\end{aligned}
$$

Next, we do the same for the moving point:

$$
\begin{aligned}
\text{AD of MovP under } \varphi \text{ of FixP} &= \sin^{-1}(\tan \delta \text{ MovP} \times \tan \varphi \text{ FixP}) \\
&= \sin^{-1}(\tan 16°55' \times \tan 51°47') \\
&= \sin^{-1}(0.30414 \times 1.27001) \\
&= 22°43'
\end{aligned}
$$

$$
\begin{aligned}
\text{OA of MovP under } \varphi \text{ of eastern FixP} &= \text{RA MovP} - \text{AD under } \varphi \text{ FixP} \\
\text{OD of Mov P under } \varphi \text{ of western FixP} &= \text{RA MovP} + \text{AD under } \varphi \text{ FixP} \\
&= 135°27' - 22°43' \\
&= 112°44'
\end{aligned}
$$

Finally, we subtract the new OA or OD of the fixed point from that of the moving point:

$$
\begin{aligned}
\text{arc of direction} &= \text{OA/OD of MovP under } \varphi \text{ of FixP} - \text{OA/OD of} \\
&\quad \text{FixP under own } \varphi \\
&= 112°44' - 106°12' \\
&= 6°32'
\end{aligned}
$$

Thus, the arc of direction for Mars conjunct Mercury *in zodiaco* by Regiomontanian circles of position is 6°32', or 6.53°. More commonly, however, the method would be used with *in mundo* positions (giving an arc of direction of 5°28', or 5.47°). Here too, some astrologers employ a hybrid variety, using *in mundo* values for the fixed but not for the moving point.

5. Calculating the Placidean Part of Fortune

Those who wish to use the mundane Part of Fortune as taught by Placidus need first of all to find the right and oblique ascensions (RA, OA) of the Moon, as well as the oblique *ascension* of the Sun, computed according to points 1 and 3 above. We shall use the chart from p. 54. (Note that oblique *ascension* is used irrespective of whether the planet concerned is in the eastern or western half of the chart.) We then determine the OA and RA of the Part of Fortune (PoF) by the following formulae:

OA PoF	= OA Asc + OA Moon - OA Sun
	= 67°58′ + 298°59′ - 126°09′
	= 240°48′

RA PoF	= OA Asc + RA Moon - OA Sun
	= 67°58′ + 246°50′ - 126°09′
	= 188°39′

If either result is negative, add 360° to it. From these values we can determine the horizontal distance (HD) and meridian distance (MD) of the Part of Fortune just as we did for a planet under points 2 and 3 above. If the 0° point on the equator (0° tropical Aries) should fall between the Part and the angle concerned, 360° must be added to the lower number.

HD in the east	= OA PoF - OA Asc
	= 240°48′ - 67°58′
	= 172°50′

If the HD is positive, the Part of Fortune is below the horizon; if the HD is negative, the Part is above the horizon. In the former case, we calculate the lower MD; in the latter case, the upper MD. Once again, if the 0° point on the equator should fall between the Part and the angle concerned, 360° must be added to the lower number.

```
upper MD   = RA PoF - RAMC
lower MD   = RA PoF - RAIC
           = 188°39' - 157°58'
           = 30°41'
```

For a Part of Fortune above the horizon, if the upper MD is positive, we add it to the HD *without any minus signs* in order to obtain the diurnal semi-arc (DSA) of the Part. But if the upper MD is negative, we subtract it from the HD (again without any minus signs) in order to obtain the DSA. For a Part of Fortune below the horizon, if the lower MD is positive, we subtract it from the HD in order to obtain the nocturnal semi-arc (NSA) of the Part. But if the lower MD is negative, we add it to the HD (without minus signs) in order to obtain the NSA.

```
DSA = HD ± upper MD
NSA = HD ± lower MD
       = 172°50' - 30°41'
       = 142°09'
```

The difference between either semi-arc and 180° will give the other semi-arc:

```
DSA = 180° - NSA
      = 180° - 142°09'
      = 37°51'
```

These semi-arcs are artificial because they do not reflect an actual diurnal motion of the Part of Fortune; they will, however, be identical with the natural semi-arcs of the Moon, if its secondary motion is disregarded. This is because the Placidean Part of Fortune is considered to share the Moon's declination.

If the RA of a Part of Fortune below the horizon is less than the RAIC, the Part is in the eastern quadrant (houses 1, 2 and 3); if its RA is greater than the RAIC, it is in the western quadrant (houses 4, 5 and 6). Conversely, if the RA of a Part of Fortune above the horizon is less than the RAMC, the Part is in the western quadrant (houses 7, 8 and 9); but if its RA is greater than the RAMC, it is in the eastern quadrant (houses 10, 11 and 12). Trisecting the relevant semi-arc will give the distance between the intermediate cusps within a quadrant – in other words, the house extension:

house extension	= SA / 3
	= 142°09′ / 3
	= 47°23′

If the MD is less than the house extension, the Part of Fortune is in the house closest to the meridian (3, 4, 9 or 10). If the MD is greater than the house extension but less than twice that arc, the Part of Fortune is in the middle house of the quadrant (2, 5, 8 or 11). Finally, if the MD is more than twice the house extension, the Part of Fortune is in the house closest to the horizon (1, 6, 7 or 12). In our example, the Part is in the 4th house.

Appendix II

Software Offering Primary Directions

An increasing range of astrological software, both commercial and non-commercial, include primary directions. The applications I have been able to examine are described below, based on the most current versions available to me.

AstroFrames

AstroFrames, developed by Ed Falis, is a no-frills, non-commercial application which correctly calculates semi-arc (Ptolemaic) directions. It offers a choice between two package solutions: positions *in zodiaco* and zodiacal aspects without latitude, or positions *in mundo* and mundane (Placidean) aspects. Either of these can be used with one of four time-keys: Ptolemy, Naibod, Cardan (0°59′12″ per year) or 'synodic' (1°00′57″ per year).

In addition to the classical aspects and planets, AstroFrames includes a number of asteroids/planetoids, which may be deselected, as well as semisquares (45°) and sesquisquares (135°), which may not. Directions against the primary motion ('converse' in the modern sense) are also included and cannot be deselected. Directions carrying a planet towards an aspect point (converse in the traditional sense), on the other hand, are not calculated at all. Lunar parallax and secondary motion are not included in the calculations.

AstroFrames was developed on Linux and has been designed to work on multiple platforms. I have examined it only on a Windows platform. AstroFrames can be downloaded from *http://mysite.verizon.net/vze6qirr/ myindex.html.*

Janus

Janus, commercial software for Windows, is a popular choice among astrologers interested in traditional techniques. Unfortunately, up to the present version (4.1) its calculations of primary directions have been seriously flawed.

The three methods of direction offered so far are labelled Alchabitius, Placidus and Mundane. The 'Alchabitius' directions, meant to be calculated by Ptolemaic semi-arcs, are miscalculated, often by several years. The 'Placidus' directions, meant to be calculated by Placidean circles of position ('under the pole'), are in fact calculated by the Regiomontanus method. Regarded as Regiomontanus directions they are correct, but only if the latitude is set to 'zero', which will in fact generate directions where the fixed element of the direction is taken *with* latitude but the moving element without it. The 'Mundane' alternative does not appear to match any known variety of primary directions. In the case of 'converse' directions in the modern sense (against the primary motion), the places of the fixed and moving elements have been reversed.

According to an announcement from the developers, these problems are being addressed in the imminent version (4.2). The 'Alchabitius' directions will be corrected and renamed Placidus semi-arc, while the current 'Placidus' directions will be known as Regiomontanus. The fixed and moving elements in the modern 'converse' directions will change places, and directing planets to aspect points (converse directions in the traditional sense) will be enabled. The current 'Mundane' option will disappear.

Janus offers a wide selection of points to be directed, including fixed stars, prenatal syzygy, some Lots or Arabic Parts, asteroids, and a number of fictive bodies. The points chosen are used as both fixed and moving elements; in other words, these cannot be chosen separately. This drawback in the design may change in the upcoming version.

There is a similarly wide selection of aspects to use, grouped in various packages. This design too may change to make aspects fully (de-)selectable. Aspect points may be taken without latitude (*in zodiaco*) or assigned the latitude of either planet involved. The latter method means that all aspect points will be located on a small circle parallel to the ecliptic and that the aspect lines or 'rays' will therefore not converge in the earth. To my knowledge this is a modern invention not used by earlier authors.

The time-keys offered are those of Ptolemy, Naibod, Brahe and Placidus. Correction for lunar parallax may be included, but not the secondary motion of the Moon.

More information on Janus is available from *http://www.astrology-house. com.*

Mercurius

Mercurius, a Windows application developed by Bernhard Bergbauer, is currently the most expensive commercial software offering primary directions. It is not, however, the best.

Directions by Ptolemaic semi-arcs (called 'Placidus') as well as Regiomontanus directions are calculated correctly, but the Placidean directions under the pole ('Placidus Kühr') are seriously miscalculated, producing hit dates which may be wrong by years. There are also directions by right ascension alone, misleadingly labelled 'Alcabitus', although in fact they are a modern invention bearing no relation to the directional methods proposed by Alcabitius/al-Qabīsī, or by any traditional author. (The attribution is based on the historically false assumption that methods of *direction* are based on systems of *house division*.)

A fifth option is called 'AlcaPlaci', again consisting of Ptolemaic semi-arcs (the method actually advocated by al-Qabīsī) with Alcabitius house cusps. Although described by the author as an 'unusual method', this was in fact the standard method used throughout the Middle Ages, when intermediate house cusps were employed at all.

The fully (de)selectable list of fixed elements (called 'significators') includes planets, angles, lunar nodes, Part of Fortune, and prenatal syzygy. The list of moving elements ('promittors') contains the same plus antiscia, planetary terms, fixed stars and the natal degrees of house cusps. The reasoning behind including intermediate cusps among the moving but not the fixed elements of a direction is not clear.

If latitude is selected, it will be used for both planets involved in the case of a conjunction, but not for points of aspect. Only the four classical aspects are included, and these are taken only in the zodiac: there are no Placidean mundane aspects. It is not possible to direct a planet to a point of aspect (converse in the traditional sense), but directions against the primary motion ('converse' in the modern sense) are included.

The only time-keys included are Ptolemy and Naibod. There is no correction for lunar parallax, nor for the secondary motion of the Moon.

More information on Mercurius is available at *http://mercurius-software. info*.

Morinus

(For the software developed by Wim van Dam, see *Morinus 2000* below.)

Morinus, developed by Robert Nagy, is a non-commercial application which far surpasses most commercial software in the field of primary directions. It offers both semi-arc and Regiomontanian directions, impressive lists of fully (de)selectable aspects and points – including planetary terms (in the tropical or sidereal zodiac), antiscia, fixed stars, and the natal degrees of ascendant and midheaven – and several other special features, such as lunar parallax correction, secondary motion of the Moon, and the Placidean (mundane) Part of Fortune. The calculations are correct, the software is easy to use and understand, and the directions are presented in a lucid and well-arranged fashion. Morinus allows directions of planets to aspect points (converse directions in the traditional sense), and directions against the primary motion ('converse' in the modern sense) may be included or excluded.

Zodiacal aspects may be calculated with or without latitude. If latitude is included, Morinus allows this to be done either by the traditional method named after Bianchini (cf. Chapter 5) or by simply assigning the latitude of a planet to all its aspects. As noted above, the latter is a modern method which leads to aspect lines converging in space rather than in the earth.

Placidean mundane aspects are also included, as are 'mundane aspects' based on the Regiomontanus and Campanus house systems. Again to the best of my knowledge, such 'aspects' were never used before the 20th century, and were certainly not advocated by either Campanus or Regiomontanus. (As both systems are based on circles of position intersecting the horizon due north and south, so-called Campanus directions will be identical to Regiomontanus, except in these mundane aspects.)

Time-keys offered are divided into 'dynamic' and 'static', the former including those of Placidus and Brahe ('true solar equatorial arc' and 'true solar equatorial arc birthday') as well as their equivalents in the ecliptic, and the latter including Ptolemy, Naibod, Cardan and a user-defined key.

The list of forthcoming features given on the website is as impressive as the rest, and includes Placidean directions 'under the pole' and rapt parallels; prenatal syzygies, hyleg, alcochoden and almuten; and profections. Even without these additions, however, Morinus is the software I would most warmly recommend to students of this book.

Morinus is designed to run on several platforms: Linux, Unix, Windows, and MacOS. I have examined it only on Windows. Morinus can be downloaded from *http://pymorinus.extra.hu*.

Morinus 2000

Morinus 2000, a commercial Windows application developed by Wim van Dam, offers correctly calculated directions by Ptolemaic semi-arcs and by Regiomontanus circles of position. The fixed element of a direction may optionally be used with latitude, but directed planets as well as aspect points are only used *in zodiaco*. Directions against the primary motion (modern 'converse') may be included, but not directions of planets to aspect points (traditional converse). An option named 'Mundane' does exist, but is an invention of the author's bearing no relation to mundane directions as commonly understood.

Fixed and moving points are selected separately from among the angles, planets, and intermediate house cusps (along with the lunar node and Part of Fortune). A great number of minor aspects may likewise be (de)selected. Correction for lunar parallax can be included, but not secondary motion.

The time-keys offered are those of Ptolemy, Naibod, Brahe and Placidus, as well as solar motion in longitude for a mean day, the birthday, or consecutive days after birth (including two modern French variations).

More information on Morinus 2000 is available at *http://astrosoftware. com/WimVanDamMorinus.htm*.

Placidus

Placidus, a commercial Windows application developed by Rumen Kolev, is undoubtedly the most advanced and versatile primary directions software on the market (although now seriously challenged by the freeware Morinus; see above). It offers a wide range of calculations, including Ptolemaic semi-arc directions, Placidean directions under the pole (as well as the 'topocentric' variation of the same), and Regiomontanian directions. For semi-arc directions, there is a free choice of which points and aspects to use; and planets may be directed to aspect points as well as vice versa.

Placidus calculates Placidean mundane aspects to planets *in mundo*, and zodiacal aspects without latitude to planets *in mundo* or *in zodiaco*. Zodiacal aspects with latitude according to Bianchini are included in some functions, and several tables, animations and 3D functions are available.

Time-keys included are those of Ptolemy, Naibod, Cardan, Brahe (here
called Kepler), Placidus, Kündig (based on the relationship between the
Sun's longitude and right ascension), solar motion in longitude for the
birthday or for consecutive days (including a variation used by van Dam;
see *Morinus 2000* above), 'synodic', and a user-defined key. All calculations
are correct, although some of the features are less easily accessible than
others, and a few can only be described as hidden away in remote corners
of the software.

The major drawbacks are in the design, which is unwieldy and visually
unattractive. There are also a few irksome and persistent flaws, such as the
inclusion of modern 'converse' directions (against the primary motion)
even when these have been deselected from the Customer Setup menu.
Lunar parallax is not calculated. There is an option of including secondary
motion for the Moon, but only in mundane directions (with Placidean
mundane aspects) and only when the Moon is the moving element (here
called 'promissor') in a direction.

The latest version of Placidus, just released, includes a new module called
Porphyrius Magus which – while adding little to the already full range of
primary directions – deserves mention here as it deals extensively with
the calculation of the hyleg and alcochoden (discussed in Chapter 9). This
module is rich in calculations based on a number of ancient and medieval
sources (with multiple choices available to the user), and potentially very
useful to astrologers interested in this branch of prediction; but it is also
graphically oppressive, and highly idiosyncratic in terms of translations
and symbols employed.

More information on Placidus is available at *http://www.babylonianastrology.com*.

Primaries.jsp

A wholly web-based, non-commercial resource is Rüdiger Plantiko's
German-language Java Server Page located at *http://www.astrotexte.ch/sources/primaries.jsp*, which correctly calculates several types of directions. In
addition to the Ptolemaic semi-arc method ('Standardverfahren'), Plantiko
offers Placidean directions under the pole of the significator ('Kühr'), the
'topocentric' variety of the same, and simplified directions in either right
or oblique ascension, or by the curious method of Goldmayer (measuring

the arcs between planetary circles of position along the prime vertical, as if the earth turned around the axis of that circle instead of its polar axis).

The fixed element of the direction (referred to as 'Signifikator' and listed first) may optionally be calculated with latitude by choosing 'Signifikator mit Breite'; the movable element ('Promissor'), whether a planet or a place of aspect, is calculated only *in zodiaco*. Mundane aspects are not included. Both fixed and moving points are offered in pre-selected packages. For the fixed points, these are: angles only ('Hauptachsen'), a 'Ptolemaic' selection (which, however, excludes the Part of Fortune, one of Ptolemy's five main significators), the seven classical planets (without the angles), or all (including non-classical planets). No planets can be deselected as moving points, but the user may choose to include only 'strong' aspects (conjunction, opposition and square), 'strong and medium' (adding trine, sextile, semisquare and sesquisquare), or all (including semisextile and quincunx). Using aspect points as the fixed element in a direction (converse in the traditional sense) is not allowed; directions against the primary motion (modern 'converse') are included by default but may be deselected by choosing 'Nur direkte Direktionen'.

There are also a number of time-keys to choose from: Ptolemy, Naibod, Cardan, Brahe ('diei motu'), Placidus ('Wahre Zeit'), Kündig, Bessler (solar motion in longitude for the birthday), Wöllner (like Ptolemy, but based on the sidereal rather than tropical year), and a 'proportional' key suggested by Plantiko himself ($0°59'18''$ per year, based on the day/year ratio applied to the degrees of right ascension in a mean solar day: $1/365.2424 \times 360°59'08''$).

Solar Fire

Solar Fire, commercial software for Windows, offers primary directions in two package solutions. The first, called Primary Mundane, calculates directions by the Ptolemaic semi-arc method, using *in mundo* positions and Placidean mundane aspects. Zodiacal aspects are not available with this option, rendering it 'more Placidean than Placidus' (who used both kinds of aspects). The directions are correctly calculated, although the information given in the user guide contains several minor errors. Placidus' preferred time-key is strangely not available for these Placidean-style directions;

instead, the Preferences menu offers a choice between the keys of Ptolemy
('1 Year per Degree'), Naibod and Brahe ('Natal Solar Rate').

The second variety, called Primary van Dam, is based on the directional
preferences of Dutch astrologer Wim van Dam (see *Morinus 2000* above),
which is to say zodiacal semi-arc directions with a key based on the Sun's
daily motion in longitude. These too are correctly calculated.

Lunar parallax and secondary motion are not included in either
package.

A problem in the design relates to how directions are presented to the
user: in the Primary Mundane package, the element of a direction carried
by the primary motion is listed first and regarded as the 'progressed point',
while the fixed element of the direction is listed second and regarded as
the 'radix point'. In the Primary van Dam package, these roles are reversed.
The user therefore needs to exercise caution to ensure, for instance, that
directions to the angles are carried out correctly by bringing the planets
and their aspect points to the horizon or meridian, rather than by assigning
aspect points to the natal angles (which, being mere points themselves,
cast no aspects).

More information on Solar Fire is available at *http://www.alabe.com*.

ZET

ZET is a commercial Windows application by Anatoly Zaytsev. English-
language versions to date (up to and including version 8) include directional
techniques which are designated as 'primary' but have little or nothing to
do with real primary directions. There is, however, a new version in the
works (currently only in Russian) which will include such directions.

At the time of going to press, the trial version calculates three varieties
of semi-arc directions. One of these is wholly *in mundo* with Placidean
mundane aspects. The other two use zodiacal aspects, giving latitude to
the fixed element (that is, taking it *in mundo*). In the first, the moving
element, whether planet or aspect point, is taken without latitude (that is,
in zodiaco) – a hybrid system. In the second, the latitude of the promissor
planet is assigned to all its aspects. As noted above, this is a modern model
which leads to aspect lines converging out in space rather than in the
earth.

Using aspect points as the fixed element in a (traditionally converse)
direction is not allowed. 'Direct' and 'converse' directions in the modern

sense (with or against the primary motion) are listed separately, and the user may choose which planets and aspects to include. The time-keys offered are Ptolemy and Naibod. Correction for lunar parallax is included, but not secondary motion.

More information on ZET is available at *http://www.zaytsev.com.*

Appendix III
The Egyptian Terms and Years of the Planets

Sign	Degrees	Ruler	Degrees	Ruler	Degrees	Ruler	Degrees	Ruler	Degrees	Ruler
Aries	0–6	Jupiter	6–12	Venus	12–20	Mercury	20–25	Mars	25–30	Saturn
Taurus	0–8	Venus	8–14	Mercury	14–22	Jupiter	22–27	Saturn	27–30	Mars
Gemini	0–6	Mercury	6–12	Jupiter	12–17	Venus	17–24	Mars	24–30	Saturn
Cancer	0–7	Mars	7–13	Venus	13–19	Mercury	19–26	Jupiter	26–30	Saturn
Leo	0–6	Jupiter	6–11	Venus	11–18	Saturn	18–24	Mercury	24–30	Mars
Virgo	0–7	Mercury	7–17	Venus	17–21	Jupiter	21–28	Mars	28–30	Saturn
Libra	0–6	Saturn	6–14	Mercury	14–21	Jupiter	21–28	Venus	28–30	Mars
Scorpio	0–7	Mars	7–11	Venus	11–19	Mercury	19–24	Jupiter	24–30	Saturn
Sagittarius	0–12	Jupiter	12–17	Venus	17–21	Mercury	21–26	Saturn	26–30	Mars
Capricorn	0–7	Mercury	7–14	Jupiter	14–22	Venus	22–26	Saturn	26–30	Mars
Aquarius	0–7	Mercury	7–13	Venus	13–20	Jupiter	20–25	Mars	25–30	Saturn
Pisces	0–12	Venus	12–16	Jupiter	16–19	Mercury	19–28	Mars	28–30	Saturn

	Sun	Moon	Mercury	Venus	Mars	Jupiter	Saturn
Greater years	120	108	76	82	66	79	57
Middle years	69½	66½	48	45	40½	45½	43½
Lesser years	19	25	20	8	15	12	30

Glossary

Terms in *italics* refer to separate entries.

abscissor	see *anaereta*
altitude	distance of a heavenly body or *ecliptical* degree above (+) or below (-) the *horizon*
anaereta	the killing planet or point in a *direction* involving the *hyleg*
anti-culmination	lowest point below the *horizon* in the *diurnal circle* of a heavenly body or *ecliptical* degree
antiscia (sg. *antiscium*)	points on the *ecliptic* holding the same *declination*, and therefore rising in the same amount of time; cf. *parallel*
apheta	see *hyleg*
arc of direction	the distance between *significator* and *promissor*, measured along the *celestial equator* or a *diurnal circle* and converted into years of life
ascendant	rising point of the *ecliptic*, marking its intersection with the *horizon* east of the *meridian*; sometimes used of the entire eastern half of the *horizon*, the rising sign, or the first house
ascensional aspect	relation between two points computed by degrees of *oblique ascension*
ascensional difference	difference between the *right ascension* and *oblique ascension* of a heavenly body or *ecliptical* degree
aspect circle	*great circle* passing through the body of a planet, used for assigning latitude to its points of aspect
axis	straight line perpendicular to the plane of, and passing through the centre of, a circle

azimuth   distance of a heavenly body or *ecliptical*
                            degree along the *horizon*, measured from
                            the latter's intersection with the *meridian*
                            in the north

celestial equator   a *great circle* in the same plane as the
                            terrestrial equator

celestial sphere   imaginary sphere of unlimited extension,
                            having the place of observation for its
                            centre, and within which all heavenly
                            bodies are positioned

circle of position   *great circle* passing through a heavenly body
                            or *ecliptical* degree, forming an artificial
                            horizon to which other points can be
                            directed

circumpolarity   the phenomenon of a heavenly body or
                            ecliptical degree neither rising nor setting

conjunctional birth   birth occurring between New Moon and
                            Full Moon

contrantiscium   point exactly opposite an *antiscium*

converse direction/motion 1. in the traditional sense, the *significator*
                            being carried by the *primary motion* towards
                            the *promissor*; 2. in the modern sense,
                            direction by an imaginary reversal of the
                            primary motion, from west to east; cf. *direct
                            direction/motion*

crepuscular space/arcs   space of astronomical twilight, 0° – 18° of
                            altitude below the horizon

culmination   highest point above the *horizon* in the
                            diurnal circle of a heavenly body or *zodiacal*
                            degree

declination   distance of a heavenly body or *ecliptical*
                            degree north (+) or south (-) of the *celestial
                            equator*

descendant   setting point of the *ecliptic*, marking its
                            intersection with the *horizon* west of the
                            meridian; sometimes used of the entire
                            western half of the *horizon*

dexter aspect	aspect in clockwise direction, backwards through the zodiac
direct direction/motion	1. in the traditional sense, the *promissor* being carried by the *primary motion* towards the *significator*; 2. in the modern sense, *direction* in the natural order of the *primary motion*, from east to west; cf. *converse direction/motion*
direction	motion of a *promissor* towards a *significator* or vice versa
diurnal arc	the part of a *diurnal circle* located above the horizon
diurnal circle	circle described by the apparent motion of a heavenly body or *ecliptical* degree around the earth from east to west during a day and night; parallel to the *celestial equator*
diurnal motion	see *primary motion*
diurnal semi-arc	half of the *diurnal arc*, delimited by the horizon and *meridian*
ecliptic	the *great circle* described by the Sun's apparent motion against the background of the fixed stars during a year
equator	see *celestial equator* and *terrestrial equator*
equinoctial	relating to the *equinox*
equinox	intersection of the *ecliptic* with the *celestial equator* in northward direction (vernal equinox, 0° Aries in the *tropical zodiac*) or in southward direction (autumnal equinox, 0° Libra in the *tropical zodiac*)
geocentric	having the centre of the earth for its centre
geocentric horizon	circle parallel to the plane of observation but having the centre of the earth for its centre; cf. *topocentric horizon*
geographical latitude	distance north (+) or south (-) of the *terrestrial equator* for a location on the earth's surface, corresponding to *declination* in the *celestial sphere*

great circle	circle within the *celestial sphere* concentric with the sphere itself
horary times	one twelfth of the *diurnal* or *nocturnal arc* of a heavenly body or *ecliptical* degree
horizon	see *geocentric horizon* and *topocentric horizon*
horizontal distance	distance of a point from the *horizon* along its own *diurnal* circle, measured in degrees of *oblique ascension*
horoscope	1. synonym of *ascendant*; 2. chart marking the positions of the heavenly bodies and *zodiac* as observed at a given time and place
hourly times	see *horary times*
hyleg	*significator* of life in a nativity
hylegiacal points	the five main *significators*: ascendant, *medium caeli*, Sun, Moon, and *Part* (or *Lot*) *of Fortune*
imum caeli	*anti-culminating* point of the *ecliptic*; its intersection with the *meridian* below the horizon
in mundo	'in the world', outside the ecliptic; see *mundane direction*
in zodiaco	'in the zodiac', on the ecliptic; see *zodiacal direction*
latitude	1. distance of a heavenly body or *ecliptical* degree north (+) or south (-) of the *ecliptic*; 2. see *geographical latitude*
longitude	distance of a heavenly body or *ecliptical* degree along the *ecliptic*, measured from 0° Aries in the *sidereal* or *tropical zodiac*
Lot of Fortune	see *Part of Fortune*
lunation	see *syzygy*
medium caeli	*culminating* point of the *ecliptic*; its intersection with the *meridian* above the horizon
meridian	*great circle* passing through the *zenith*, *nadir*, and north and south points of the *horizon*

meridian distance	distance of a point from the *meridian* along its own *diurnal circle*, measured in degrees of *right ascension*
midheaven	see *medium caeli* (upper midheaven) or *imum caeli* (lower midheaven)
mundane aspect	relation between two points based on proportions of their respective *semi-arcs* in the different *quadrants* of the chart
mundane direction	*direction* of points not located on the *ecliptic*
mundane parallel	relation between two points, one fixed and the other moving, distant from the *horizon* or *meridian* by the same proportion of their respective *semi-arcs*
nadir	point on the *celestial sphere* exactly below the place of observation
nocturnal arc	the part of a *diurnal circle* located below the *horizon*
nocturnal semi-arc	half of the *nocturnal arc*, delimited by the *horizon* and *meridian*
oblique ascension	point on the *celestial equator* rising simultaneously with a heavenly body or *ecliptical* degree
oblique descension	point on the *celestial equator* setting simultaneously with a heavenly body or *ecliptical* degree
obliquity of the ecliptic	angle of inclination between the *ecliptic* and the *celestial equator*, caused by the tilt of the earth's rotational axis in relation to the plane of its orbit around the sun; currently about 23°26′
obscure space/arcs	space of darkness, located below the *crepuscular* space
ortive difference	difference between the *horizontal distances* of two points located at the same *altitude* below the *horizon*

parallax	difference in apparent position of a heavenly body (most notably, the Moon) when viewed from different locations (cf. *geocentric horizon* and *topocentric horizon*)
parallel	1. parallel of *declination*, circle on which all points rise in the same amount of time (cf. *antiscia*); 2. see *mundane parallel*
paranatellonta	fixed stars or planets rising simultaneously with another point, typically an *ecliptical* degree
Part of Fortune	calculated point derived by projecting the distance between the Sun and Moon from the ascendant
partile aspect	1. in the earlier sense, aspect occurring between degrees bearing the same ordinal number; 2. in the later sense, aspect occurring within a distance of 60′ of arc
polar circles	circles of *geographical latitude* (derived by subtracting the *obliquity of the ecliptic* from 90°) beyond which parts of the *ecliptic* become *circumpolar*
pole	terminal point of an *axis*; when used of a planet, the axis is that of its *circle of position*
precession	cyclical change in the direction of the earth's polar axis, resulting in a regression of the equinoxes through the fixed constellations, each complete cycle lasting approximately 25,800 years; see *sidereal zodiac* and *tropical zodiac*
preventional birth	birth occurring between Full Moon and New Moon
primary motion	the apparent daily motion of the *celestial sphere* (and hence the *zodiac* and all heavenly bodies) from east to west, caused by the rotation of the earth around its axis from west to east

prime vertical	*great circle* passing through the *zenith*, *nadir*, and east and west points of the *horizon*
primum mobile	'first movable': in pre-modern cosmology, the outermost of the spheres thought to revolve around the earth, sometimes identified with the zodiac
promissor	active element of a *direction*, determining the nature of the event; generally a planet, aspect, or fixed star
promittor	see *promissor*
prorogator	see *hyleg*
quadrant	quarter-part of the *celestial sphere* (and, secondarily, of all *diurnal circles*) delimited by the *horizon* and *meridian*
RA	see *right ascension*
RAIC	the *right ascension* of the *imum caeli*, where the *meridian* intersects the *celestial equator* below the *horizon*
RAMC	the *right ascension* of the *medium caeli*, where the *meridian* intersects the *celestial equator* above the *horizon*
rapt motion	see *primary motion*
rapt parallel	relation between two moving points, distant from the *horizon* or *meridian* by the same proportion of their respective *semi-arcs*
right ascension	location of a heavenly body or *ecliptical* degree along the *celestial equator*, measured from the vernal *equinox*
right direction/motion	see *direct direction/motion*
secondary motion	apparent motion of a planet along the *zodiac*, caused by the orbits of the planet and the earth around the Sun
sect	group of planets (and occasionally other points) considered to have an affinity either with the Sun and daytime (diurnal sect) or with the Moon and nighttime (nocturnal sect)

semi-arc	part of a *diurnal circle*, delimited by the *horizon* and *meridian*; cf. *quadrant*
sidereal zodiac	*zodiac*, defined in relation to one or more fixed stars, through which the *equinoxes* regress
significator	passive element of a *direction*, determining the area of life affected; generally an angle, planet (particularly the Sun or Moon), or Part/Lot
sinister aspect	aspect in anti-clockwise direction, forwards through the zodiac
synanatellonta	see *paranatellonta*
syzygy	exact conjunction or opposition of the Sun and Moon (New or Full Moon, respectively); sometimes also used of their squares
temporal aspect	see *ascensional aspect*
terrestrial equator	imaginary circle perpendicular to the earth's axis of rotation and dividing the earth into a northern and a southern hemisphere
topocentric	having the place of observation for its centre
topocentric horizon	*great circle* forming the plane of observation with a place on the surface of the earth for its centre; cf. *geocentric horizon*
tropical zodiac	*zodiac*, defined in relation to the *equinoxes*, through which the fixed stars progress
vernal equinox	see *equinox*
zenith	the point on the *celestial sphere* exactly above the place of observation
zodiac	belt of some 9° of *latitude* to either side of the *ecliptic*, divided equally into the twelve signs beginning with Aries
zodiacal direction	*direction* between points located exactly on the *ecliptic*

Bibliography

Modern editions and translations of classical texts are listed under the name of the editor/translator. The abbreviation *s.a.* means *sine anno* (no year); *s.l.* means *sine loco* (no place). For modern reprints, years of first publication of the originals are given in square brackets.

Abenragel
    1551   *Albohazen Haly filii Abenragel libri de iudiciis astrorum.* Basilea [Basel].

Beck, R.
    2007   *A Brief History of Ancient Astrology.* Oxford.

Bishop, J. and Kirby, R.
    1687   *The Marrow of Astrology.* London. [Reissued in 1688 under the sole name of Bishop.]

Burnett, C. et al.
    2004   *Al-Qabīṣī (Alcabitius): The introduction to astrology: editions of the Arabic and Latin texts and an English translation.* London.

CCAG 8.4
    1921   *Catalogus Codicum Astrologorum Graecorum*, vol. 8, part 4, ed. P. Boudreaux and F. Cumont. Bruxellis [Bruxelles].

Cooper, J.
    2004   *Primum Mobile [...] by Didacus Placidus de Titus.* [1814] S.l.

Curry, P.
    1992   *A Confusion of Prophets: Victorian and Edwardian Astrology.* London.

Dykes, B.
    2007   *The Book of Astronomy by Guido Bonatti.* Golden Valley, Minnesota.
    2008   *Works of Sahl & Māshā'allāh.* Golden Valley, Minnesota.

Gauricus, L.
    1557   *Tabulae de Primo Mobili.* Roma [Rome].

Greenbaum, D. G.

2001   *Late Classical Astrology: Paulus Alexandrinus*
                       and Olympiodorus with the Scholia from Later
                       Commentators. Reston, Virginia.

Hand, R. S.

1995a   *Antonius de Montulmo: On the Judgment of*
                       Nativities. Parts I–II. Berkeley Springs, West
                       Virginia.

1995b   *Night & Day: Planetary Sect in Astrology.* Reston,
                       Virginia.

1996   *Johannes Schoener: Opusculum astrologicum.* [First
                       ed. 1994.] Berkeley Springs, West Virginia.

1997   *Omar of Tiberias: Three Books on Nativities.*
                       Berkeley Springs, West Virginia.

Holden, J. H.

1994   *Astrologia Gallica Book Twenty-Two: Directions.*
                       Tempe, Arizona.

1996   *A History of Horoscopic Astrology.* Tempe,
                       Arizona.

2002   *Astrologia Gallica Book Twenty-Three: Revolutions.*
                       Tempe, Arizona.

2004   *Astrologia Gallica Book Twenty-Four: Progressions*
                       and Transits. Tempe, Arizona.

2008a   *Astrologia Gallica Book Sixteen: The Rays and*
                       Aspects of the Planets. Tempe, Arizona.

2008b   *Astrologia Gallica Book Seventeen: The Astrological*
                       Houses. Tempe, Arizona.

2008c   *Sahl ibn Bishr: The Introduction to the Science of*
                       the Judgments of the Stars. Tempe, Arizona.
                       2008d *Abu ʿAli al-Khayyat: The Judgments of*
                       Nativities. [First ed. 1988] Tempe, Arizona.

Howe, E.

1968   *Astrology: A recent history including the untold*
                       story of its role in World War II. New York. [Original
                       title: *Urania's Children,* 1967.]

Hübner, W.

1998   *Claudii Ptolemaei opera quae exstant omnia,* vol.
                       III.1: Αποτελεσματικα. Lipsiae [Leipzig].

Knappich, W.
   1935   'Placido de Titi's Leben und Lehre' in *Zenit*,
                       7–11.
Knobloch, E. and Schönberger, O.
   2004   *Vettius Valens: Blütensträusse*. St. Katharinen.
Kolev, R.
   s.a.   *Primary Directions I: Directions to MC, IC, ASC. &
                       DESC*. Varna.
   2008   *Greek & Arab Astrology: Hyleg, Alchocoden &
                       Almuten*, part I. Varna.
Kühr, E. C.
   1936   *Berechnung der Ereigniszeiten*. Görlitz in
                       Schlesien.
Kunitzsch, P.
   1977   *Mittelalterliche astronomisch-astrologische Glossare
                       mit arabischen Fachausdrücken*. München.
Leo, A. (F. W. Allen)
   1923   *The Progressed Horoscope*. [First ed. 1906.]
                       London.
Lilly, W.
   1659   *Christian Astrology: Book III*. [First ed. 1647.]
                       London.
   1822   *William Lilly's History of his Life and Times*. [1715]
                       London.
Makransky, M. J.
   1992   *Primary Directions: A Primer of Calculation*.
                       Occidental, California. [Digital version.]
Neugebauer, O. and Van Hoesen, H. B.
   1959   *Greek Horoscopes*. Philadelphia.
North, J. D.
   1986   *Horoscopes and History*. London.
Oxley, T.
   1830   *The Celestial Planispheres, or Astronomical Charts*.
                       London.
Partridge, J.
   1693   *Opus Reformatum*. London.
   1697   *Defectio Geniturarum*. London.

Pearce, A. J.
 2006   *The Text-Book of Astrology*. [1911] Tempe,
                Arizona.
Pingree, D.
 1976   *Dorothei Sidonii Carmen astrologicum*. Leipzig.
 1978   *The Yavanajātaka of Sphujidhvaja*, vol. II.
                Cambridge, Massachusetts.
 1986   *Vettii Valentis Antiocheni anthologiarum libri
                novem*. [Edition of the Greek text.] Leipzig.
Placidus de Titis
 1675   *Physiomathematica, sive Coelestis Philosophia*.
                Mediolanum [Milan].
Plantiko, R.
 1996   *Primärdirektionen: Eine Darstellung ihrer Technik*.
                Mössingen. [Published digitally.]
Regulus
 2008   *A Rectification Manual: The American Presidency*.
                Princeton, New Jersey. [Anonymous work
                published digitally by Regulus Astrology LLC,
                2007; revised edition 31 October, 2008.]
Robbins, F. E.
 1940   *Ptolemy: Tetrabiblos*. Cambridge, Massachusetts.
Sachau, E. C.
 2002   *Albêrûnî's India*. [1888] New Delhi.
Schmidt, R.
 1993   *Antiochus of Athens: The Thesaurus*. Berkeley
                Springs, West Virginia.
 1994   *Vettius Valens: The Anthology, Book III*. Berkeley
                Springs, West Virginia.
 1995   *Claudius Ptolemy: Tetrabiblos, Book III*. Berkeley
                Springs, West Virginia.
Sepharial (Old, W. R.)
 2006   *Primary Direction: A Definitive Study*. [1915]
                Bel Air, Maryland. [Original title: *Directional
                Astrology*.]
Sibly, E.
 1826   *A New and Complete Illustration of the Celestial
                Science of Astrology*. [1784 – 1790] London.

Strauß, H. A. and Strauß-Kloebe, S.

    1981   *Die Astrologie des Johannes Kepler: eine Auswahl aus seinen Schriften.* [1926] Fellbach-Oeffingen.

White, T.

    1810   *The Beauties of Occult Science Investigated; or, The Celestial Intelligencer.* London.

Wilson, J.

    2006   *A Complete Dictionary of Astrology.* [1819] Bel Air, Maryland.

Worsdale, J.

    1828   *Celestial Philosophy, or Genethliacal Astronomy.* Lincoln.

Wright, R. R.

    2003   *The book of instruction in the elements of the art of astrology / by Abu'l-Rayḥān Muḥammad ibn Aḥmad al-Bīrūnī.* [1934] London.

Zahel

    1519   *De significatione temporis* [included in *Liber quadripartitus Ptolomei*]. Venecia [Venice].

INDEX

A

Abdilaziz, see: al-Qabīṣī ʿAbd al-ʿAzīz
Abenragel, see: ʿAlī ibn Abī r-Rijāl
Abraham ibn Ezra, 62, 63
abscissor, see: anaereta
Abū ʿAlī al-Khayyāṭ, 17, 30, 62
Abū Maʿshar, 1, 29, 68
aktinobolia (ἀκτινοβολία), 7
al-Bīrūnī, 9, 18, 31, 47, 63
Alcabitius, see: al-Qabīṣī ʿAbd al-ʿAzīz
Alcabitius houses, ii, 47, 56, 59–60,
    63, 64, 112, 163
alcochoden, 118–119, 128, 132, 164, 166
Alexandria, ii, 117
algerbuthar, see: divisor
al-Hamdānī, 68, 72
ʿAlī ibn Abī r-Rijāl, 5, 9, 10, 63–64, 68,
    70, 72, 99, 105
al-jānbaḫtān, al-jānbaḫtār, see: divisor
al-Jayyānī, 63
al-kadḫudāh, see: alcochoden
al-Manṣūr, 16
al-Qabīṣī ʿAbd al-ʿAzīz, 18, 31, 56, 63,
    143, 163
al-qāsim, see: divisor
altitude, 35, 42, 46, 95–96, 121
anaereta, *anairetēs* (ἀναιρέτης), 109,
    111, 112–113, 117, 118, 120–121,
    124, 126, 131, 132
angles, 1, 5, 8, 18, 24, 48, 51, 52, 53,
    59, 61, 70, 80, 91, 92, 98, 103,
    105,115, 125, 139
antiscia, 91–92, 118, 130, 163, 164
Antonio de Montulmo, 19, 31
Aomar, see: ʿUmar aṭ-Ṭabarī
aphesis (ἄφεσις), 11, 27, 106
apheta, *aphetēs* (ἀφέτης), see: hyleg

aphetic points, see: hylegiacal points
Arabic, 11, 16, 17, 18, 27, 30, 31, 106,
    118, 119, 129, 132
Arabic astrology, see: Perso-Arabic
    astrology
Arabic Parts (Lots), 7, 17, 97, 162;
    see also: Part of Fortune
ar-Rijāl, see: ʿAlī ibn Abī r-Rijāl
ascendant, 1, 2, 4–6, 12, 13, 16, 17,
    21, 27, 42, 44–45, 48–52, 54,
    60, 61, 62, 66, 67, 70, 71, 77, 80,
    85, 92, 97, 98–100, 105, 107–108,
    110, 113, 114–116, 118, 121,
    124, 125, 128, 129, 132, 133,
    134,136–137, 139, 141–142,143,
    144, 146
aspect circle, 69–70, 162, 164, 165
aspects, 3, 4, 6, 8, 12–13, 16, 17, 30,
    50, 51, 62, 64, 65–68, 70–71, 72,
    77–78, 80, 87, 95, 96, 97, 98–99,
    107–108, 109–110, 111, 115,
    118–119, 124, 126–127, 128, 130,
    131, 137, 139, 140, 141, 145
    ascensional or temporal, 89,103
    dexter/sinister, 7, 67–68
    with latitude, 50, 59, 68–70, 72,
        76, 87, 133, 162, 164, 165;
    mundane, 23, 50, 90–91, 94, 97,
        99, 102, 103, 125, 133, 160, 164,
        165, 167;
    new varieties invented, 23, 76, 88,
        102, 103
athazir, at-tasyīr, see: tasyīr
ayanāṃśa, ii
azimuth, 35, 41–42, 43, 46, 64

B
Baghdad, 16
Balbillus, 11, 28, 116–117, 131
Benedictus XVI, see: Ratzinger,
    Joseph
benefics and malefics, 23, 30, 52, 62,
    67–68, 70–71, 72, 109–111, 114–115,
    121, 123–124, 126–127, 128,
    131, 132
Besant, Annie, 100–101
Bianchini, Giovanni, 69, 87, 164, 165
biodotēr (βιοδοτήρ), see: divisor
Bishop, John, 22, 32, 103
Blanchinus, see: Bianchini, Giovanni
Bonatti, Guido (Bonatus), 18
bounds, see: terms
Brahe, Tycho, 74–75, 79, 80
Byzantine Empire, 16, 116, 131

C
Campano, Giovanni (Campanus), 47
Campanus house system, 37, 59,
    112–113
Cardano, Gerolamo (Cardan), 19, 31, 80
Carmen astrologicum, see: Pentateuch
Catholicism, 21–23, 77, 119
celestial sphere, i, 6, 7, 9, 33–34, 37,
    46, 94, 98
circle of position, 56, 58–59, 94–95;
    see also: pole of planets
circumpolarity, 40–41
clime, 13
Coley, Henry, 21, 32
Collectio Geniturarum, 22
converse motion, see: direct and
    converse motion
crepuscular arcs, 95–96, 102, 103,
    121, 132
Cromwell, Oliver, 22
cum latitudine, 50
    see also: in mundo

D
death, 13, 17, 19, 24, 31, 50, 62, 106,
    111, 113, 118, 119–121, 123–124,
    125–127, 128
decan (face), 118, 132
declination, 38, 40–41, 43, 46, 92, 94,
    97, 104, 132, 140
Defectio Geniturarum, 22, 32
descendant, 1, 4, 42, 45, 49, 61, 92,
    107, 109–111, 115, 118, 125
dexter aspect, see: aspect
direct and converse motion, 7, 8, 10,
    17, 67–68, 71, 92, 99–100, 104,
    105, 109, 110, 111, 121–122, 127;
    modern reinterpretation of, 24,
        31, 83, 98–101, 102, 142, 144
directio, 11, 27
diurnal arc, 43–45, 46, 53, 60, 91, 92,
    110, 115, 143
diurnal circle, 43–45, 46, 48, 58, 59,
    61, 65, 82, 91, 95, 122
diurnal directions, 143, 145
divisor, 17, 27
Dorotheus of Sidon, 1, 11–13, 17, 18,
    28, 68, 106, 130, 132
Dykes, Benjamin, 30–31, 132

E
ecliptic, 4, 18, 34, 39–43, 45, 46, 49,
    50, 52, 60, 61, 62, 63, 65, 69, 71, 80,
    82, 89–90, 91–92, 97, 98, 104
equator
    celestial, 13–14, 34, 37–39,
        40, 41, 43, 44, 45, 46, 57, 59, 89–90,
        92, 94, 104
    terrestrial, 5, 30, 36, 37, 94
equinoxes, 29, 38, 39, 40, 43, 44, 130,

F
face, see: decan
fixed and moving elements of
    direction, 5–7, 8, 17, 61, 67–68, 71,
        80, 82, 84, 95–96, 142

fixed zodiac, see: sidereal and tropical zodiacs
Fortune, see: Part of Fortune

G
Gadbury, John, 21–22, 32
Gaurico, Luca, 105
geocentric horizon, see: horizon
great circle, 5, 34, 37, 39, 41, 43, 46, 57–58, 69, 82, 84, 94
Greek, ii, 11, 16–17, 23, 27, 29, 103, 106–107, 109, 118, 129
Gustav II Adolf (Gustavus Adolphus), 119–122, 132

H
hairesis (αἵρεσις), see: sect
Haly Abenragel, see: ʿAlī ibn Abī r-Rijāl
Hand, Robert, 28, 30, 103, 129
haylāj, see: hyleg
Hellenistic astrology, 7, 9, 11, 15–16, 29–30, 72, 97, 107, 117–118
Hephaestio of Thebes, 130, 132
hīlāj, see: hyleg
Hindu astrology, see: Indian astrology
Hipparchus, 29
Hogendijk, Jan P., 10, 63
Holden, James Herschel, 15, 25, 28, 29, 30, 31, 70
horia (ὅρια), see: terms
horizon, 1, 3–4, 5–6, 12–13, 15, 27, 29, 34–44, 46, 48–49, 52–53, 57–58, 59–60, 61, 62, 63, 64, 65, 66, 77, 83, 84, 86, 89, 91–92, 94, 95–96, 98, 102, 104, 105, 107–108, 110, 113, 118, 121, 122, 124, 126, 128, 129, 142; geocentric and topocentric, 35, 83
horizontal distance, 96
House of Wisdom (Bayt al-Ḥikma), 16
house systems, ii, 1, 9, 19, 25, 37, 41, 47, 56, 57, 59–60, 61, 62, 63, 64, 91, 94, 105, 107, 112–113, 116, 123, 142, 163, 164
hyleg, 10, 24, 30, 64, 68, 72, 106–127, 128, 129–133, 140
hylegiacal points, 5, 16

I
imum caeli (IC), 1, 15, 45, 49, 54, 61, 118, 125
Index of forbidden books, 21
Indian astrology, 11, 9, 16, 29, 31, 107, 129
ingresses, 140–143, 145, 146
in mundo directions, 50–52, 53, 56, 59, 61, 62, 63, 69, 83, 88, 92, 97, 103, 104, 113, 123
intermediate house cusps, 1, 9, 56, 57, 59–60, 61, 63–64, 70, 91, 103, 105, 112, 113, 121, 142, 144, 163
in zodiaco directions, 25, 50–53, 59, 61, 62, 80–81, 83, 113

J
Jupiter, 49, 51, 62, 66–68, 72, 77–78, 80, 94–95, 109, 110–111, 113, 120–121, 124, 127, 130, 136, 137, 139, 141, 142, 143
Justus van Gent, i

K
Kepler, Johannes, 80, 88
'keys', 73–78, 79, 80, 81, 85, 113, 121, 137, 142, 143
Kirby, Richard, 22, 103
Knappich, Wilhelm, 25
Knobloch & Schönberger, 130, 132
Königsberg, 19
Krishnamurti, K. S., ii
Kühr, Erich Carl, 9, 25, 86–87, 94, 141–144, 145, 146
Kunitzsch, Paul, 129

L

Latin, ii, 9, 11, 16, 17, 18, 19, 23, 27, 30, 31, 37, 47, 69, 72, 106, 109, 118, 119, 129, 132

latitude
   celestial, 17-18, 22, 39, 41-42, 45, 46, 50, 52, 59, 61, 63, 65, 68-70, 71, 72, 76, 78, 85, 87, 88, 97, 104, 109, 124, 127, 133, 162, 164, 168
   geographical, 13, 37, 40-41, 44, 89, 94

Leo, Alan (W. F. Allen), 24-25, 99, 101

Leon the Philosopher, 130

Liber Astronomiae, 18

life-span, 7, 11, 12, 16, 18, 19, 24, 50, 72, 80, 97, 106-127, 128, 131, 140

Lilly, William, 1, 5, 21-23, 27, 57, 67, 74, 79, 88, 103, 105, 134-135

Lindh, Anna, 125-127, 133

longevity, see: life-span

longitude, 4-5, 17, 30, 39, 41, 46, 50, 52, 54-55, 61, 62, 65, 66, 70, 83, 89, 92, 110, 131, 146

Lot of Fortune, see: Part of Fortune

Lots, see: Arabic Parts

lunar return, see: revolution

lunation, see: syzygy

M

Magini (Maginus), 70, 75, 90

Makransky, M. J., 63

malefics, see: benefics and malefics

Mars, ii, 2, 12, 14, 19, 31, 50, 51-52, 53-56, 58-59, 64, 67-68, 72, 73, 77, 81, 109, 110, 113, 117, 120-122, 124, 126-127, 131, 133, 135-136

Māshāʾallāh, 1, 17, 29, 30

medium caeli (MC), 1, 5, 15, 21, 27, 28, 37, 44-45, 49, 50, 51, 61, 67, 70, 77-78, 81, 92, 98-99, 101, 105, 109, 114, 115, 118, 120-121, 125, 126, 135-136, 139, 141-142, 146

Mercury, 13, 19, 31, 53-56, 58-59, 66, 73, 109, 110, 115, 124, 126

meridian, 6, 15, 28, 34, 36-39, 41-44, 46, 48, 49, 52, 53, 57, 59, 61, 63, 65, 73, 83, 84, 91, 92, 94, 98, 100, 142

midheaven
   lower, see: *imum caeli*
   upper, see: *medium caeli*

Μικροπαναστρων (*Mikropanastrōn*), 21

moderator, see: significator

Moon, 3-6, 16, 19, 21, 23, 27, 31, 39, 41-43, 48, 52-53, 62, 70, 76, 82-85, 86, 87, 91, 94, 97, 99, 102, 104, 105, 107-108, 109, 113, 114, 115, 116, 118, 121, 124, 126-127, 128, 129, 131, 132, 139, 140, 141, 144, 145

Morin de Villefranche, Jean-Baptiste, i, 1, 5, 9, 19-22, 25, 27, 57, 62, 69-70, 74, 75-76, 79, 80, 83, 87, 88, 92, 97, 99, 105, 119-121, 134, 138-139, 141, 144, 145, 146

Morrison, Richard James (Zadkiel I), 24, 32, 94

moving zodiac, see: sidereal and tropical zodiacs

Müller, Johann; see: Regiomontanus

mundane direction, see: *in mundo*

N

nadir, 35-37, 40, 46

Naibod, Valentin, 74, 75, 80

nature, planetary, 2, 8, 9, 13, 17, 52, 53, 62, 71, 72, 76

Nechepso, 106

Negusanti, Adriano, 97, 104

Neptune, 89, 142

Neugebauer & Van Hoesen, 131-132

nocturnal arc, 43-45, 46, 91-92, 110

O

oblique ascension/descension, 29,
38–39, 96, 104, 105
aspects in oblique ascension, 89,
103
directions in oblique ascension, 28
obliquity of the ecliptic, 39–41, 43
obscure arcs, 95–96, 102, 103
oikodespotēs (οἰκοδεσπότης), see:
alcochoden
Old Master painting, i
Old, Walter Richard (Sepharial),
24–25, 94, 104, 105
Omar Tiberiades, see: 'Umar aṭ-Ṭabarī
Opus Reformatum, 21–22, 32
Oxley, Thomas, 99, 103, 104, 105

P

Pahlavi, 11
parallax, 35, 83–85, 86, 87, 88
parallel
of declination (zodiacal, see also:
antiscia), 91–92, 97, 104, 132,
140
mundane and rapt, 9, 92, 97, 102,
122, 124
Part of Fortune, 5, 16, 21, 27, 70,
107–108, 112, 116, 124, 128, 132,
139
mundane definition of, 97, 102, 104
Partridge, John, 21–23, 28, 32, 94, 98,
103, 104, 129, 132
Paul of Alexandria, 14
Pearce, Alfred James (Zadkiel II),
24–25, 31, 32, 94, 103, 105
Pentateuch, 11, 130
Persian, 16, 17, 106, 118, 129, 132
see also: Pahlavi
Perso-Arabic astrology, 9, 16–18, 24,
27, 29, 63, 97
Petosiris, 15, 106
Phoenix, River, 49–50, 62

Physiomathematica, 21
Pico della Mirandola, 19, 31
Pingree, David, 28, 129
Placidus (Placido de Titi), 1, 11,
19–21, 22, 23, 24, 27, 31, 32, 56,
70, 75, 80, 83, 87, 88, 90–91, 92,
93–94, 95–96, 97, 99, 102, 103, 104,
119, 121–123, 124–125, 128, 132,
133, 134, 139–140, 141–142, 145
Placidus houses, 25, 56, 59, 62, 91,
112, 123, 142
Plantiko, Rüdiger, 63
Pluto, 89
pole, 63
of the earth, 36, 37, 41
of planets, 25, 93–94, 102, 104, 122,
142
see also: circle of position
Porphyry houses, 47, 112
Portwood, Samuel, 123–124
precession, ii, 29, 138–139
primary directions, use and meaning
of term, 1–2, 11
primary motion, 1–2, 6–7, 8, 10, 12,
24, 31, 39, 53, 57, 65, 74, 79, 80, 87,
92, 95, 98, 101, 102, 103, 105, 109–
110, 111, 123, 127, 128, 141, 142,
143, 144
prime vertical, 34, 37, 41, 59, 63
primum mobile, 9, 91–92
profections, 20, 134–137, 138, 139,
140, 141, 145
progressions, 11, 20, 25, 27, 31,
139–140, 145
see also: secondary directions
promissor (promittor), 5–6, 7, 8, 9,
15, 17–18, 67–68, 71, 77, 79, 80,
82–83, 84, 89, 92, 97, 98–99, 124,
127, 135, 137, 139, 141, 143, 145
proportional semi-arcs, 30, 52–56,
61, 78, 82–83, 91, 92–96, 103, 127,
131, 132, 142

see also: Ptolemaic directions
prorogator, see: hyleg
Protestantism, 21, 23, 119
Ptolemaic directions, 16, 18, 20–21,
    27, 56, 61, 91, 93, 102, 103, 117,
    119, 122, 124, 128, 140, 142
Ptolemy, Claudius, i, 1, 5, 7, 10, 15–16,
    17, 18, 19–23, 27, 29–30, 31, 39, 53,
    56, 57, 70, 73, 85, 79, 82, 89, 91,
    97, 103, 106–111, 113, 115–116,
    117–118, 119, 121, 124, 125–127,
    128, 129–130, 131, 134, 140

Q
quadrant, 91, 94, 115
    houses, ii, 1, 112–113
Quadripartite, 23, 119
    see also: Tetrabiblos

R
radix, 2, 30, 70, 71, 86–87, 134, 137,
    138, 139, 141, 142, 143, 144, 145
Raphael, see: Smith, Robert Cross
rapt motion, 97
    see also: primary motion
rapt parallel, see: parallel, mundane
    and rapt
Ratzinger, Joseph (Benedict XVI),
    75, 77–78, 137, 139, 143, 146
rectification, 52, 61, 80, 120, 129
refraction, 83–84, 85, 86, 88
Regiomontanus, 1, 19, 27, 56–57, 59,
    61, 63, 70, 94
Regiomontanus houses, 25, 56–57,
    59, 62–63, 93, 105, 112
retrograde planets, 7, 10, 39
revolution
    lunar, 139, 141, 144, 145, 146
    solar, 62, 138–140, 141, 143–144,
        145, 146
Rhetorius the Egyptian, 63
right ascension, 5, 15, 28, 38–39, 43, 46,

49, 50, 54–55, 57, 58, 67–68, 73–75,
79, 82, 94, 104, 110, 115, 122, 146
    aspects in, 90
    directions in, 163
right motion, see: direct and
    converse motion
rising times, 5, 13–18, 27, 89, 92, 114,
    115, 117, 131

S
Sahl bin Bishr, 17, 30, 31
Sanskrit, 129
Saturn, 13, 19, 50, 72, 76, 77, 109,
    110, 113, 116, 117, 120–122, 124,
    126–127, 131–132, 133, 141, 143
Schmidt, Robert, 130
Schöner, Johann, 9, 19, 31
secondary directions (progressions),
    11, 20, 24, 25, 27, 80, 139–140, 145,
    146
secondary motion, 39, 46, 53, 65, 73,
    74, 82–83, 84, 85, 86, 88, 103, 122,
    140, 141, 145
sect, 62, 66, 107–108, 121, 126, 129–130
Sepharial, see: Old, Walter Richard
sidereal and tropical zodiacs, ii, 16,
    29–30, 31, 39, 43, 47, 91, 112 130,
    138–139
significator, 5–7, 8, 9, 12, 13, 15, 16,
    21, 27, 30, 62, 66, 67–68, 70, 77, 79,
    82–83, 84, 89, 91, 92, 93, 97, 98–99,
    134–135, 137, 139, 140, 141, 143,
    144, 145
    of life, see: hyleg
Simmonite, William Joseph, 24
sinister aspect, see: aspect
size, of solar and lunar disks, 84–85,
    86, 88
Smith, Robert Cross (Raphael), 24
solar return, see: revolution
Stand By Me, 50
Sun, 1, 5, 14, 16, 21, 23, 27, 31, 37, 38,

39, 41, 43, 45, 46, 49–50, 53, 62, 66,
70, 73–75, 77–78, 79, 80, 84, 86,
91, 92, 94, 95–96, 97, 99, 102, 103,
104, 107–108, 109, 112–113, 114,
116, 118, 121–122, 123–124, 127,
128, 129, 131, 132, 137, 138–139,
140. 142, 143, 145, 146
syzygy,   116, 118, 132

T
tājika,   129
    see also: Perso-Arabic astrology
tasyīr,   10, 11, 27, 143–144
terms (bounds),   12–13, 17, 23–24,
    27, 28, 65, 77, 108, 109, 111, 113,
    115, 116, 118, 123, 124, 126, 130,
    131, 132, 133
tertiary directions,   32, 140
Tetrabiblos,   15, 23, 29, 30, 57, 106, 119,
    129, 130
Thrasyllus,   116
topocentric horizon, see: horizon
transits,   135, 138–139, 140–143, 145
trigonometry,   i–ii, 21, 53
triplicity,   108, 111, 118, 126, 130
Troinski, Edmund Herbert,   31, 140
tropical zodiac, see: sidereal and
    tropical zodiacs

U
ʿUmar aṭ-Ṭabarī,   16–18, 30, 68, 132
Uranus,   89, 100–101, 142

V
Venus,   2, 12–13, 28, 62, 64, 67–68, 69,
    72, 92, 103, 109, 110, 124, 127, 130,
    136
Vettius Valens,   14, 16, 110, 113–115,
    117, 131, 132

W
Washington, George,   80
western astrology,   ii, 1, 8, 22, 25, 29
    term questioned, 9
Western Roman Empire,   16
Wilson, James,   99, 103, 104
Worsdale, John,   22–24, 28, 94, 99,
    103, 104, 105, 123–124, 133

Z
Zadkiel I, see: Morrison, Richard
    James
Zadkiel II, see: Pearce, Alfred James
zenith,   35–37, 40, 46, 94
zodiac,   1, 4–5, 6–7, 133–14, 27, 28,
    37, 38, 39–41, 43–45, 46
    see also: sidereal and tropical
        zodiacs
zodiacal direction, see: *in zodiaco*
zodiacal parallel, see: parallel of
    declination

Other Books by The Wessex Astrologer

The Essentials of Vedic Astrology
Lunar Nodes - Crisis and Redemption
Personal Panchanga and the Five
Sources of Light
Komilla Sutton

Astrolocality Astrology
From Here to There
Martin Davis

The Consultation Chart
Introduction to Medical Astrology
Wanda Sellar

The Betz Placidus Table of Houses
Martha Betz

Astrology and Meditation
Greg Bogart

Patterns of the Past
Karmic Connections
Good Vibrations
Soulmates and why to avoid them
Judy Hall

The Book of World Horoscopes
Nicholas Campion

The Moment of Astrology
Geoffrey Cornelius

Life After Grief - An Astrological Guide
to Dealing with Loss
AstroGraphology - The Hidden link
between your Horoscope and your
Handwriting
Darrelyn Gunzburg

The Houses: Temples of the Sky
Deborah Houlding

Temperament: Astrology's
Forgotten Key
Dorian Geiseler Greenbaum

Astrology, A Place in Chaos
Star and Planet Combinations
Bernadette Brady

Astrology and the Causes of War
Jamie Macphail

Flirting with the Zodiac
Kim Farnell

The Gods of Change
Howard Sasportas

Astrological Roots:
The Hellenistic Legacy
Joseph Crane

The Art of Forecasting
using Solar Returns
Anthony Louis

Horary Astrology Re-Examined
Barbara Dunn

Living Lilith - Four Dimensions of the
Cosmic Feminine
M. Kelley Hunter

Your Horoscope in Your Hands
Lorna Green

www.wessexastrologer.com

Lilly significatus p 5

Rule

P7 dexter (aspect) (square)

Angles

solar arc direction

p23 - diurnal arc

p23 - Terms

p30 - mundo

whole sign?
Gounds?